(re)union

a STUDY GUIDE

for SEEKERS, SAINTS,

and SINNERS

BRUXY CAVEY

HERALD
P R E S S

Harrisonburg, Virginia

Herald Press
PO Box 866, Harrisonburg, Virginia 22803
www.HeraldPress.com

**Designed to be used with *Reunion: The Good News of Jesus
for Seekers, Saints, and Sinners,* 978-1-5138-0130-8, $16.99 USD.**

Scriptures taken from the *Holy Bible, New International Version*®, NIV®. Copyright © 1973,
1978, 1984, 2011 by Biblica, Inc.™ Used by permission of Zondervan. All rights reserved
worldwide. www.zondervan.com The "NIV" and "New International Version" are trade-
marks registered in the United States Patent and Trademark Office by Biblica, Inc.™

REUNION: A STUDY GUIDE
© 2018 by Bruxy Cavey
Released by Herald Press, Harrisonburg, Virginia 22803. 800-245-7894.
All rights reserved.
International Standard Book Number: 978-1-5138-0252-7
Printed in United States of America
Cover and interior design by Reuben Graham

24 23 22 21 20   14 13 12 11 9 8 7 6 5

CONTENTS

LETTER FROM BRUXY

Dear reader,

You're diving in! I'm so glad. No message is worthier of our focused, unhurried attention than the gospel: the good news of Jesus for seekers, saints, and sinners.

The good news of Jesus is about reunion with God. This relationship is a *re*union, because it is about coming home—about getting back to something and Someone we left behind but who has never left us alone. The gospel is also about moving forward into a new and deeper *union* unlike anything humankind has experienced before. It's a union made possible by God becoming one of us through Jesus, bonding with us, living and loving and suffering alongside us, and then taking our humanity with him back up into union with God's love life. When we are "in Christ," which is a major theme in the Bible, we are in intimate union with God. What good news, that this life of reunion with our Maker stretches into eternity—and even better, that it can start right here, right now. That is the good news of Jesus.

WE'RE ALL IN THIS TOGETHER

This study guide, which is designed to be used with the companion book *Reunion* (see information at the back of this book), will help you dig deeper into this life-changing message of Jesus, whether you are a spiritual seeker, a churchgoing saint, or a broken sinner—or, like I am, all three. The apostle Paul wrote *to Christians* in Rome that he was eager to preach the gospel to them because the gospel not only has the power to save but also provides light for living (see Romans 1:14-17). Paul also wrote *to Christians* in Corinth, "Now, brothers and sisters, I want to remind you of the gospel I preached to you, which you received and on which you have taken your stand" (1 Corinthians 15:1). The early church knew the importance of an ongoing ministry of reminding. Through practices like baptism and the eucharist (also called communion or the Lord's Supper), as well as through letters of encouragement and regular meetings for teaching, discussion, and prayer, the early Christians always found ways to *remind themselves* of the gospel, not just preach it to others.

And the apostle Peter wrote *to Christians* who already knew the gospel, "So I will always remind you of these things, even though you know them and are firmly established in the truth you now have. I think it is right to refresh your memory as long as I live in the tent of this body, because I know that I will soon put it aside, as our Lord Jesus Christ has made clear to me. And I will make every effort to see that after my departure you will always be able to remember these things" (2 Peter 1:12-15). Here is a powerful truth: growing spiritually will always include a ministry of reminding. In other words, the gospel of Jesus is a message for everyone, Christians and non-Christians alike. The good news of Jesus is not just a message that sinners are saved by; it is a message that saved people live by.

One beautiful application of this truth is that Christians and not-yet-Christians, seekers and skeptics, the dedicated and the doubtful can all study the gospel, learn from Jesus, and take their next steps to grow spiritually *together*. And this study guide is designed to help you do exactly that.

TALK ABOUT FAITH: YOU'RE KIDDING, RIGHT?

If you are not a Christ-follower, I'm hoping this study will help you decide if you want to become one. Nothing could be more important. Pardon me for a moment, though, while I address something with committed Christians. For you Christians, I'm hoping this book study will help you learn how to talk—that's right, *talk*—about your faith in Jesus with non-Christians.

Many of us Christians claim our favorite quotation on the topic of evangelism comes from Saint Francis of Assisi: "Preach the gospel at all times. When necessary, use words." Great quote, right? Except for two problems. First . . . he never said it. At least, we have no record of Saint Francis saying it. Nevertheless, *someone* said it, and we love it. I think we love it because it justifies our "quiet in the land" approach to evangelism . . . which is to say, not evangelizing at all.

And that's the second problem with this beloved quotation: *it is always necessary to use words when preaching the gospel.* The good news of Jesus is a message, with actual content, that is meant to be communicated—it is good *news*.

Sometimes Christians will reason, "I evangelize through how I live. I live a good life, and people see and experience the love of Jesus through me." To this sentiment I say three things: First of all, let's be clear: it *is* good to live a good life. (Duh!) Second, living a good life is not evangelization; it is simply living a good life. And third, a question: Are you really so confident that you live such an uncommonly good life that people watch you and say, "I must know more about the God who is obviously at work in that person's life"? Hopefully, every Christ-follower is growing more Christlike. But most of us have a long way to go before we arrive at the finished project.

Now here's something Saint Francis *did* say: "It is no use walking anywhere to preach unless our walking is our preaching." His point is this: don't go out of your way to *give* the gospel if you aren't committed to *live* the gospel. Amen. But this call away from hypocrisy and toward authenticity is not intended to justify our common refusal to simply, genuinely, and authentically talk about our faith in Jesus. Jesus is our example. In the ministry of Jesus, we both *see* the presence of the kingdom and *hear* the proclamation of the kingdom. A radically loving life should come with an explanation. And any proclamation of the gospel should be accompanied by a radically loving life. It's not either/or, but both/and.

If we almost never talk about Jesus with our friends and family, we can't use the excuse of "Well, I'm just letting my life be my witness." Yes, we want our walk to match our talk. But that works both ways. We need our *talk* to match our *walk*!

In fact, if we almost never talk about Jesus with people around us, it may be that we are creatively, systematically, and subconsciously avoiding the topic. Otherwise, if Jesus is so important to us, he should come out naturally in all kinds of friendly conversation. If Jesus is our first love, our primary mentor, and the teacher who most shapes our thinking on all kinds of relational topics, how could we not quote him? How could we not at least reference him in conversations from time to time . . . unless we're consciously or subconsciously trying not to?

For instance, say you are married. If your friends, family, coworkers, and neighbors have no idea you are married because you never mention your spouse at all, I'd say you are doing your spouse—and others—a disservice. Honoring the person who is most important to us is not just about how we treat them when we're alone together, but about how (or if!) we represent them when we're around other people. Part of any basic, friendly relationship is being open and authentic about what is most important to us.

Here's another example: If you and I were friends for years, or even just months, and you still had no idea how much I love lawn bowling, you would be right. Because I don't. Never have.

But if you had no idea how much I love Thai food, dancing, and scary movies (not at the same time, but now that you mention it, what a great idea!), I would have to say you don't know me that well at all yet. In fact, if we've been friends for months and you don't know these most basic things about what makes me tick, then I probably need to do some self-assessment. I'd need to ask, why am I avoiding talking about these basic qualities and affections that make up a key part of who I am? We naturally talk about the people and things we are most excited about. If you're not talking about Jesus naturally and regularly with people around you, then something is, well, off.

So if we have been intentionally, even if subconsciously, avoiding talking about Jesus in our everyday relationships, some retraining may need to happen. What should be a natural way of being in this world—talking about Jesus in regular conversation—will feel unnatural at first, like learning to walk again after muscles have atrophied because of injury.

For those of us who need a little evangelism rehab, here are some ways that we might naturally bring up Jesus in conversation (although with intentional effort at first, remember). Try relating what you know about Jesus to the variety of topics you cover in everyday conversations by using some of these kick-start phrases:

- "That reminds me of a story Jesus told . . ."
- "That reminds me of a teaching of Jesus . . ."
- "That reminds me of something Jesus did . . ."
- "That reminds me of something the Bible says about Jesus . . ."
- (Baby-steps version) "That reminds me of something I learned at church recently . . ."
- (Babier-steps version) "That reminds me of something in this book I'm reading called *Reunion* . . ."

Of course, if we're going to say things like this, we have to be people who actually pay attention to the things Jesus taught and did. We need to read the Gospels (Matthew, Mark, Luke, and John) and think about the teaching and example of Jesus. We need to read the rest of the Bible with Jesus in mind. And we will certainly benefit by attending church, reading books, listening to podcasts, reading blog posts, and engaging in conversations with an alertness for what we can learn about and from Jesus.

For some of us Christians, maybe *this* is the problem. We don't actually live lives immersed in the person, teaching, life, and lessons of Jesus. Let's be honest: *that's* why we don't talk about him.

If this sounds like you, the good news is that by participating in this book study, you're already making changes. I, for one, am very excited for what lies ahead for you.

I'M PRAYING FOR YOU

I may be the most excited one of the bunch—that you are working your way through this study together. I'll be praying for you and with you and would love to hear from you if and when you get underway. For now, I'd love to join you in a prayer:

Dear God,

Thank you for the privilege of this time, this place, and being with these people to focus on Jesus together.

Spirit of God, we invite you to be our teacher, to speak to our hearts as well as our minds.

Jesus, may your light shine in us and among us.

Amen.

Bruxy

HOW TO USE THIS STUDY GUIDE

This study guide is more than discussion questions for chapters in *Reunion*; it also provides some new thought-provoking content for discussion. Each session may provide more material than is possible to discuss together in the time you have. Discussion leaders can decide what to focus on and what to leave for the keeners to pursue individually (*keeners* is Canadian talk for eager beavers—wait, is that Canadian talk too?).

Regardless of whether you are using this study guide for personal reflection, group discussion, or classroom content, I hope that your *learning* becomes *living*, and that your living becomes an act of *giving* the gospel away, with clarity and compassion.

SUGGESTIONS FOR LEADERS
If you are leading a group discussion of *Reunion* with this study guide, here are some suggestions.

- Structure the time to serve your needs. Some groups might want to start with a meal, or at least have snacks and drinks available.
- Start each session with prayer, asking God to be your teacher.

- Review the appropriate chapter or chapters from *Reunion* together. Take your time with this part, and invite everyone to help rebuild your collective memory of the content. Remember that people are busy, and some may come to the meetings having not done the required reading. Taking time for group members to review and remind each other of the content of each week's reading can be a good refresher for everyone. The questions listed in the "Hang Out" section will be helpful for this.

- Each session is divided into three parts: Hang Out, Hear, and Huddle.

  1. **Hang Out:** [30 minutes-ish] Keep your group together for this section and enjoy some initial conversation as a large group. This part of the session is meant to get the mind and the group dynamics warmed up. You might want to consistently start with these open-ended questions: What do you think was the main point of the chapter or chapters? What idea stood out to you personally? What questions did the reading raise for you? (Don't get sidetracked by trying to answer all questions at this point. Answers may come in future chapters. It's just worth giving group members an opportunity to voice their questions.) Sometimes these initial conversations are the most important. This section also provides some extra thoughts to read and a brief video to watch. But don't move on to this new material without first reviewing what participants have already read in the book and making time for their thoughts and questions.

  2. **Hear:** [30 minutes-ish] Now it's time to see how specific passages of the Bible connect with the core message of the gospel. We want to share our opinions and hear from one another, yes, but most importantly, we want to hear from God. The questions in this section are an opportunity to share personal opinions, but most of all they should serve to help the group better understand the text of Scripture. Remind people that these passages are worth becoming extra-familiar with, and some people may even want to memorize all or parts of them. At the very least, there is a "Remember" section with a suggested passage to commit to memory. For the "Study" section, if your group has more than six or eight people, feel free to reorganize

into smaller discussion groups. That way more people can have the chance to participate verbally. Then come back together and have the groups report on thoughts they found helpful or lingering questions they have.

3. **Huddle:** [15 minutes-ish] This is the chance for participants to make it personal. You may want to break up into huddle groups of three to five people. (Once a huddle hits six people, you've really got two huddles of three.) While the "Study" groups in the "Hear" section might mix up members each week, you could decide to keep the huddles consistent to help build deeper friendships and to allow for comfortable sharing. Give these huddle groups time to talk more personally about things they are learning and what God might be saying to them. If appropriate for the people attending, take time to pray for each other. (Note: Huddles may or may not suit your group. They are meant to help people process the "So what?" question in applying the material to their lives. That process is important, but it may not be where everyone is at.)

- Don't try to do it all! You don't need to discuss every question or follow every conversational train of thought to the end of the line. Think of the questions and other ingredients in each session as a kind of menu: they are there to serve you and not the other way around. Use what you can and leave the rest for individuals to return to later.

- Note that the questions are designed to allow non-Christians, new Christians, and long-time Christians to study together. People may need time to adjust, however, depending on the makeup of the group and the comfort level with each other. Emphasize that we're all seekers, saints, and sinners, and we're all walking the path toward God together.

PREPARING FOR THE FIRST SESSION

The first session is a doozy! Participants are asked to come prepared to discuss the first five chapters of *Reunion*, including the gospel in one word and three words! Yes, this is a lot of up-front reading, but it serves a purpose. This allows the pace to slow down and the discussion to dig deeper for the rest of the sessions, which focus on the gospel in thirty words.

The leader can, of course, choose to break up the first session over multiple weeks. But we've found that eight weeks is a good length for these kinds of studies, which means you'll need to cover more up front. Make sure participants get a copy of the book in plenty of time to do the reading before the first session.

THE STUDY BUDDY OPTION

"When we teach, we learn" observed Seneca the Younger, a Roman philosopher who lived around the same time as Jesus. There is something about organizing our thoughts enough to communicate them to someone else that helps us learn more than if we simply study as a student. Psychologists call it "the protégé effect," observing that students who tutor other students are the ones who learn the most.

Want to grow the most through this process? Then take the protégé effect—the idea that we learn when we teach—one step further through the *Reunion* study buddy program. This isn't just for leaders but is for anyone in the group—and that means you!

Here's the idea: ask one person who isn't part of this discussion group if they would be willing to be your study buddy for the next eight weeks. This would entail your study buddy being willing to talk with you—in person, on the phone, or online—for about five to ten minutes each week. The purpose of this discussion is to *give you the opportunity to teach them what you are learning and receive their feedback.* You're not trying to change their thinking as much as simply inviting them to give you feedback about your clarity as a communicator of this content.

Your study buddy could be someone who already believes in the good news of Jesus, but a nonbeliever could be especially helpful in assisting you to be clear about concepts that might be new to them. Are you making sense? Do you know the material? Are you making it easy to understand? Helping them understand will help you understand—*capisce*?

Remember: your study buddy doesn't have to agree with you at the end of the conversation! You are asking for feedback on how *you* explain the content, not on *their* agreement with it. There is no need to debate or argue about different points of view (unless you both want to). And you don't have to have answers for all your study buddy's questions, so don't get sucked into trying to be an authority, and don't be intimidated. Remember, you're not trying to win an argument, and you're not trying to convert them! (Nor should they be trying to convert you!) Being your study buddy is just a gift they can give you: when you try to communicate clearly what you are currently learning and they give you feedback, they are actually helping *you* learn.

What do you say? Do you think you're up for it? Look for the "Study buddy talking points" in each session for ideas. And contact a friend or family member soon to ask them to be your study buddy!

BRAND NEW

That time you got together
with a group to talk about Jesus

» Read chapters 1–5 of *Reunion* before this session «

👥 HANG OUT

In this session we're laying the foundation for our understanding of the message Jesus proclaimed and embodied. Because Jesus didn't just deliver God's Word to us but *is* the Word of God to humankind, the good news *of* Jesus will always focus *on* Jesus. If we don't get this straight first, everything else will be harder to grasp. God has a message for this world—and his name is Jesus.

Some people's faith starts with God in general. They have a feeling that God exists and an idea about what God might be like, and that's a fine place to start. But this approach doesn't guarantee that we will get to know the *true* God. Is it Yahweh? Allah? Brahma? Gaia? Or something or someone else we have yet to consider? Knowing *that* God is—that is important. Knowing *who* God is and *what* God is like—that is paramount.

While praying to the Father, Jesus said, "Now this is eternal life: that they know you, the only true God, and Jesus Christ, whom you

Jesus came to show us what God is like, and to help us know that God accurately and intimately.

have sent" (John 17:3). Jesus came to show us what God is like, and to help us know that God accurately and intimately. Without Jesus, our knowledge of "God" will be at best incomplete, and at worst, full of bad ideas.

Is God personal, so that we can have a relationship together? Or is God impersonal, like an energy field that I can learn to manipulate to accomplish what I want? Is God distant, detached, and untouched by human suffering? Or is God interested, involved, and intimately engaged with the most raw, painful, and beautiful parts of our human experience? Is God easily angered, offended, and quick to judge? Or is it God's love that always has the last word in every situation?

Speaking of Jesus, the apostle Peter wrote, "Through him you believe in God, who raised him from the dead and glorified him, and so your faith and hope are in God" (1 Peter 1:21). Did you catch that? *Through Jesus we believe in God.* Rather than saying "I'll start by deciding if I can believe in God based on other evidence (e.g., philosophical arguments, the fine tuning of the cosmos, the reported experiences of others, etc.), and if I do, then I'll work on figuring out which religion has God's approval," Peter recommends a better way. We start with Jesus, and he will lead us to the truth about God's existence and God's essence.

Left to my own thoughts and my best assessment of the evidence around me, I am rather agnostic about the existence of God. But when I study the teachings and life and love of Jesus, I am convinced that Jesus is trustworthy and true—and Jesus tells me there is a God and what that God is like! Like the apostle Peter said, through Jesus I believe in God.

NOTES

_____

_____

_____

_____

_____

_____

Starting with Jesus not only helps us believe that God exists, but also helps us know what God is like, right from the start. Our starting point will often determine how we filter everything else we learn about God. When we don't start with God's Word—Jesus—we will often have a lot to unlearn before we can learn the truth of the God Jesus called Father.

The apostle Paul wrote, "For though we live in the world, we do not wage war as the world does. The weapons we fight with are not the weapons of the world. On the contrary, they have divine power to demolish *strongholds*. We demolish *arguments* and every *pretension* that sets itself up against the *knowledge* of God, and we take captive every *thought* to make it obedient to Christ" (2 Corinthians 10:3-5, emphasis mine). Paul is referring to bad ideas about God that people hear and hold on to and that get in the way of really knowing God. Philosophical arguments, pretentious speculations, or just massive memes of misinformation—these can become like intellectual strongholds, military bases of bad ideas. And one thing a study like this can equip us to do is to demolish, to tear down some of the bad ideas that have kept us captive for much of our lives.

> *Starting with Jesus helps us know what God is like*

ASK

1. We've come to this first session having read a lot of *Reunion*. What stood out to you from chapters 1–5, either as an encouragement, a challenge, a disagreement, or a question?

2. This is a book for seekers, saints, and sinners. Which group do you identify with most? Why?

NOTES

3. Some people think Jesus is being unnecessarily narrow or divisive when he says things like, "I am the way and the truth and the life. No one comes to the Father except through me" (John 14:6). How does the book address this? What do you think?

4. Sometimes people refer to followers of any of the three great monotheistic religions—Judaism, Christianity, and Islam—as "People of the Book." How is this true and yet not true of people who follow Jesus?

5. Philosopher Marshall McLuhan coined the phrase "The medium is the message." How does this apply to Jesus?

6. Dynamite plus particleboard is not more but less. Jesus plus other additives is not better but worse. What other ideas, philosophies, or religions are you prone to mix with the good news of Jesus? How do they affect your understanding of the gospel?

WATCH

Take a few minutes to watch this brief video to help prepare you for this week's discussion.[1]

ᴵᵗᴵˡᴵ HEAR

It's time to hear from God through Scripture. A bit of background before you read: the word *covenant* means a relational contract, or a way of being and living together. The old covenant given through Moses is about God's way of being with humankind before Jesus, which was based on law-keeping and ritual sacrifice. This old covenant of rules,

---

1. bruxy.com/reunionstudy1

NOTES

_____

_____

_____

_____

_____

_____

rituals, and routines was a kind of exoskeleton, an external framework to help hardhearted people live better lives. When children are young and strong-willed, they need clear routines and firm rules. But God always promised that one day he would establish a new covenant that would change everything and help humanity grow up. Through the new covenant, God would soften our hard hearts and give his own Spirit to each person to partner with us in living loving lives.

Hundreds of years before Jesus was born, the Bible records these words of the prophets.

God always promised that one day he would establish a new covenant that would change everything

READ

Jeremiah 31:31-34

[31] "The days are coming," declares the Lord,
  "when I will make a new covenant
  with the people of Israel
  and with the people of Judah.
[32] It will not be like the covenant
I made with their ancestors
  when I took them by the hand
  to lead them out of Egypt,
  because they broke my covenant,
  though I was a husband to them,"
  declares the Lord.
[33] "This is the covenant I will make with the people of Israel
  after that time," declares the Lord.

NOTES

_____

_____

_____

_____

_____

"I will put my law in their minds
    and write it on their hearts.
I will be their God,
    and they will be my people.
[34] No longer will they teach their neighbor,
    or say to one another, 'Know the Lord,'
    because they will all know me,
    from the least of them to the greatest,"
    declares the Lord.
"For I will forgive their wickedness
    and will remember their sins no more."

Ezekiel 36:25-27

[25] I will sprinkle clean water on you, and you will be clean; I will cleanse you from all your impurities and from all your idols. [26] I will give you a new heart and put a new spirit in you; I will remove from you your heart of stone and give you a heart of flesh. [27] And I will put my Spirit in you and move you to follow my decrees and be careful to keep my laws.

Joel 2:28-29

[28] And afterward,
    I will pour out my Spirit on all people.
Your sons and daughters will prophesy,
    your old men will dream dreams,
    your young men will see visions.
[29] Even on my servants, both men and women,
    I will pour out my Spirit in those days.

NOTES

_____

_____

_____

_____

_____

STUDY

1. What verse or idea stands out to you the most from these Scripture passages? Why?
2. What are some of the characteristics of the promised new covenant? How are these qualities different from those of the old covenant that God gave Israel through Moses? Given these differences, why is the new covenant good news?
3. How does Jesus—his life and death and life again—bring about the new covenant?
4. The new covenant includes the promise of a new heart and a new spirit, as well as God's own Spirit in us. Have you experienced this? If so, talk about the difference it makes. If not, discuss your questions about this promise.

REMEMBER

"I will give you a new heart and put a new spirit in you" (Ezekiel 36:26).

 # HUDDLE

1. What do you sense God might be saying to you through the material discussed this week?
2. If your huddle group is open to it, take time to pray for each other, that we all might learn, live, and give the gospel.

STUDY BUDDY TALKING POINTS

If you haven't done so already, make sure you explain the purpose of being a study buddy to the person you've invited to become yours. You

NOTES

_____

_____

_____

_____

_____

aren't asking them to debate with you or suggesting that you can answer all their questions. You simply want to get their feedback on how clear you are while you share what you're learning. This weekly commitment doesn't need to last longer than five to ten minutes, although of course you're free to chat as long as you like.

First, take a few minutes to learn about your study buddy's spiritual views. It will be good to know their views, learn from them, and have some context for whatever you share. Then share what you're learning. If you need help, here are some suggestions.

- What do you think about this idea: Human spirituality functions more like a kite than a balloon. Our spirits soar highest when attached to a guiding hand, rather than when we cut all ties. What, if anything, are you attached to for spiritual guidance and growth?
- What is your spiritual or religious background and history? How would you describe your spiritual beliefs today? One last question: What comes to mind when you think about Jesus?
- The message of Jesus to the world is called "the gospel," which means good news. It is good news because it makes very clear that God is good and loves us like crazy.
- Jesus also brought an end to the old way of religion, with its morality based on a law ethic (outside-in living), and taught his followers how to live according to a new love ethic (inside-out living).
- Jesus is God's message to us—God's show-and-tell. Becoming and being students of Jesus is how we can become the best version of ourselves.

NOTES

SESSION 2

GOD WITH US

The most dangerous good news ever

» Read chapter 6 of *Reunion* before this session «

👥 HANG OUT

Welcome back! In this session we're digging deeper into the implications of the profound reality that the Creator became his creation through Jesus. As one of us, God made it clear that our Maker is for us and not against us. Theologians call this the incarnation, or what we have called the *ground* of the gospel (see The Gospel in Thirty Words, p. 27).

Jesus was prophesied to be Immanuel, or "God with us" (Matthew 1:23). And because God is with us that is, for us and not against us—being in right relationship with God will meet all our fundamental human needs. We'll be talking about this idea in this and future sessions. But first, a word of caution.

During World War II, Nazi soldiers had the phrase "Gott mit uns" (God with us) inscribed on belt buckles and rings. Clearly, believing that God is on our side is not a guarantee that we will live loving lives. In fact, history proves precisely the opposite. Believing that God is on

Being in right relationship with God will meet all our fundamental human needs.

our side—that God is with us—can be a recipe for disaster and destruction. That's because sometimes we interpret it as saying that God is *not* with the other side. When misunderstood and improperly applied, the idea of Immanuel (God with us) can embolden our sectarian violence rather than extinguish it.

God with us. Dangerous words—unless that God says he is with *all* of us, on *all* our sides, together. *This* is the message Jesus came to proclaim and embody and empower us to live.

Centuries before Christ, when an angel bearing a sword appeared to Joshua the warrior just before the battle of Jericho, Joshua asked the angel, "Are you for us or against us?" To which the angel replied, "Neither. I'm on the Lord's side" (my paraphrase; see Joshua 5:13-15). We can't hijack God's message of universal love to make it serve our own agenda and still leave the gospel intact. In the first century when Jesus was born, it would have been possible for Jewish people who were being oppressed by the Romans to hear "God with us" as the promise of God being *with* them, specifically, and therefore *against* their oppressors. But Jesus, whose life defines the idea of Immanuel, would grow up to teach that God is with us and for us *all*. God is for us, and therefore he wants us to experience maximum human flourishing, to see those who bear his image and likeness thrive in this world.

> We can't hijack God's message of universal love to make it serve our own agenda.

Over the next few sessions, as we work through the gospel in thirty words, take note of the ways each aspect of the gospel connects with a fundamental human need, both for our good and for our growth.

NOTES

THE GOSPEL IN THIRTY WORDS:

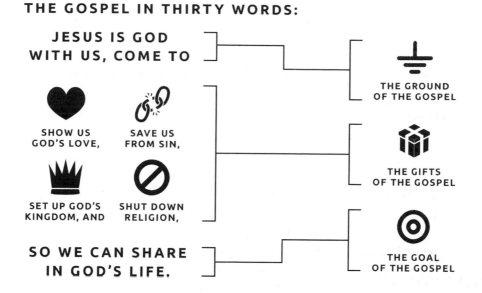

JESUS IS GOD WITH US, COME TO

SHOW US GOD'S LOVE,

SAVE US FROM SIN,

SET UP GOD'S KINGDOM, AND

SHUT DOWN RELIGION,

SO WE CAN SHARE IN GOD'S LIFE.

THE GROUND OF THE GOSPEL

THE GIFTS OF THE GOSPEL

THE GOAL OF THE GOSPEL

Speaking of human needs: most people who have taken first-year psychology are at least somewhat familiar with Abraham Maslow's hierarchy of needs. Abraham Maslow (1908–1970) first published his famous hierarchy of needs in 1943, and revised it just before his death in 1970.[1] Maslow pointed out that the most basic physiological needs (like food, water, and sleep) must be met before we can progress toward meeting our deeper human needs (such as belonging and esteem). For example, if you are dying of thirst, or if you don't know where you're going to sleep

---

1 A. H. Maslow, *The Farther Reaches of Human Nature* (New York: Viking, 1971). Maslow has been critiqued for leaving out "purpose" or "meaning" in life as a fundamental human need, so we've added it into this version. This list of human needs otherwise represents his thinking entirely.

NOTES

_____

_____

_____

_____

_____

_____

tonight, focusing on your sense of self-esteem or self-actualization will be difficult. But once we have our basic physiological needs met, we will then naturally progress to seek out solutions for our higher human needs.

Maslow's list isn't perfect, and it's certainly not exhaustive. Even Maslow himself criticized and adjusted his own work later in life (good for him!). Nevertheless, Maslow's hierarchy of needs can serve as a kind of kick start to get us thinking about what matters to us most, and about how the gospel addresses our most fundamental human needs (start at bottom of chart below).

MASLOW'S HIERACHY OF FUNDAMENTAL NEEDS

SELF-TRANSCENDENCE (SHARE IN GOD'S LIFE)

SELF-ACTUALIZATION (SHUT DOWN RELIGION)

PURPOSE (SET UP GOD'S KINGDOM)

ESTEEM (SAVE US FROM SIN)

BELONGING (SHOW US GOD'S LOVE)

SAFETY/SECURITY (GOD WITH US)

PHYSIOLOGICAL NEEDS (AIR, FOOD, WATER)

Now let's reflect again on the gospel in thirty words and see how each aspect meets one of the deepest needs of the human heart.

There is a lot here that we won't unpack in this session. We'll come back to this in later weeks. But for now, I'll make three initial observations.

First, people sometimes assess the truth of Jesus by discussing evidence for his miracles, especially his resurrection. If Jesus really did heal the sick, walk on water, change the weather, cast out demons, and rise from

NOTES

_____

_____

_____

_____

_____

_____

the dead, he must be who he claimed to be. Providing evidence for faith is called *apologetics*. I'd like to suggest that one of best approaches to apologetics available to us is the actual teaching of Jesus. Christ's greatest miracle is his message and how the message of Jesus addresses our most fundamental human needs. The fit between our most fundamental human needs and the solution Jesus offers is, dare I say, miraculous. Let's keep this in mind as we progress through this study in the weeks ahead.

Second, although the gospel in thirty words doesn't *directly* address physiological needs (which Maslow said must be met first), history has shown that a community of people who learn and live the gospel will work together to serve the poor and provide for their physiological needs and beyond. After all, Jesus referred to his message and mission this way:

> The Spirit of the Lord is on me,
>> because he has anointed me
>> to proclaim *good news to the poor*.
> He has sent me to proclaim freedom for the prisoners
>> and recovery of sight for the blind,
>> to set the oppressed free,
>> to proclaim the year of the Lord's favor.
> (Luke 4:18-19, emphasis mine)

It is no coincidence that the vast majority of compassion organizations that work tirelessly to bring water to the thirsty and food to the hungry, to provide medical care to the sick and comfort to the dying, are Christian organizations and church-sponsored programs. If we're going to follow Jesus, we're going to follow him straight into places of poverty.

Third, the message of "God with us" (Matthew 1:23) is foundational for humans to feel safe and secure in this universe. God, the Creator

NOTES

_____

_____

_____

_____

_____

_____

and Sustainer of all things, is really with us. That is, God is for us and not against us. And God has entered our human history to provide us tangible evidence that this is so. When we allow this truth to sink in, it opens us up to being ready to trust the rest of the message. Without this initial sense of security and safety with God, God's power and glory may fill us with dread, and we will never get beyond our fear—fear of judgment, fear of failure, fear of rejection—to hear the rest of the message. "God with us" is God's way of saying to all of us: "Fear not" (see, for example, Matthew 28:10; Luke 1:30; 2:10; and John 14:27).

While reflecting on the gospel, the writer of the book of Hebrews says, "Let us then approach God's throne of grace with confidence, so that we may receive mercy and find grace to help us in our time of need" (Hebrews 4:16). With confidence! Some translations say "with boldness." Because of Jesus, we can come to God and the gospel with bold confidence that God is for us and not against us. And our ears are open to hear the rest of the message.

ASK

1. What stood out to you from chapter 6 of *Reunion*, either as an encouragement, a challenge, a disagreement, or a question?
2. Have you ever talked with someone who believes there are many paths up the mountain to God? Or maybe you have wondered the same thing. What do you think about this chapter's response to that idea (pp. 72–73 in *Reunion*)?
3. Have you ever seen, heard, or used one of the truncated, incomplete versions of the gospel (pp. 68–70 in *Reunion*)? What are their strengths? Weaknesses?

NOTES

4. Why do you think popular gospel presentations emphasize salvation from sin but not the kingdom of Christ lived in the world today?

5. "I believe that one reason you're reading this book right now is because of the activity of the Holy Spirit in your life. You have never been without the Spirit's influence. He has been with you all along as a voice of conviction and encouragement, patiently moving you toward Jesus" (p. 76 in *Reunion*). What do you think about this idea? Reflecting on your life (or even just on how you came to be reading this book and study guide), can you sense times when God has been at work in your life?

WATCH

Take a few minutes to watch this brief video to help prepare you for this week's discussion.[2]

ᛁᛁᛁ HEAR

It's time to hear from God through Scripture. When the Word of God became human, we were all given an unprecedented and unparalleled opportunity to see the character of God like never before or since. Read these Bible passages about our unique opportunity to see God by looking at Jesus, and the result of being made confident that God is for us, not against us.

---

2. bruxy.com/reunionstudy2

NOTES

_____

_____

_____

_____

_____

_____

READ
John 1:1-18 (excerpts)

¹ In the beginning was the Word, and the Word was with God, and the Word was God. ² He was with God in the beginning. ³ Through him all things were made; without him nothing was made that has been made. ⁴ In him was life, and that life was the light of all mankind. ⁵ The light shines in the darkness, and the darkness has not overcome it. . . .

⁹ The true light that gives light to everyone was coming into the world. ¹⁰ He was in the world, and though the world was made through him, the world did not recognize him. ¹¹ He came to that which was his own, but his own did not receive him. ¹² Yet to all who did receive him, to those who believed in his name, he gave the right to become children of God— ¹³ children born not of natural descent, nor of human decision or a husband's will, but born of God.

¹⁴ The Word became flesh and made his dwelling among us. We have seen his glory, the glory of the one and only Son, who came from the Father, full of grace and truth. . . .

¹⁶ Out of his fullness we have all received grace in place of grace already given. ¹⁷ For the law was given through Moses; grace and truth came through Jesus Christ. ¹⁸ No one has ever seen God, but the one and only Son, who is himself God and is in closest relationship with the Father, has made him known.

John 5:37-40

³⁷ And the Father who sent me has himself testified concerning me. You have never heard his voice nor seen his form, ³⁸ nor does his word dwell in you, for you do not believe the one he sent. ³⁹ You study the Scriptures diligently because you think that in them you have eternal life. These are the very Scriptures that testify about me, ⁴⁰ yet you refuse to come to me to have life.

NOTES

Colossians 1:15-23

[15] The Son is the image of the invisible God, the firstborn over all creation. [16] For in him all things were created: things in heaven and on earth, visible and invisible, whether thrones or powers or rulers or authorities; all things have been created through him and for him. [17] He is before all things, and in him all things hold together. [18] And he is the head of the body, the church; he is the beginning and the firstborn from among the dead, so that in everything he might have the supremacy. [19] For God was pleased to have all his fullness dwell in him, [20] and through him to reconcile to himself all things, whether things on earth or things in heaven, by making peace through his blood, shed on the cross.

[21] Once you were alienated from God and were enemies in your minds because of your evil behavior. [22] But now he has reconciled you by Christ's physical body through death to present you holy in his sight, without blemish and free from accusation— [23] if you continue in your faith, established and firm, and do not move from the hope held out in the gospel.

(Also see Hebrews 1:3; 2:14–3:6; and 4:14-16.)

STUDY

1. What verse or idea stands out to you the most? Why?
2. Recall the theme of last session's video: that God's Word is Jesus, and the Bible points to him. So if you miss the Jesus focus of Scripture, you're missing the Word of God. That seems to be what Jesus is saying to religious leaders in John 5. Even though they knew Scripture exceptionally well, Jesus tells them, "You have never heard his voice . . . nor does his word dwell in you" (John 5:37-38). Talk about how Jesus should change the way we read the Bible, especially when it comes to: (a) rituals, (b) rules, and (c) violence.

NOTES

_____

_____

_____

_____

_____

_____

3. Jesus is Immanuel (God with us, God for us and not against us). If this is true, we should expect to see this in how Jesus taught, lived, and died. Think of some examples from the life and teaching of Jesus that drive this point home.

4. In Colossians 1, the apostle Paul says we were alienated from God "in [our] minds" but now we can live "free from accusation." How does the good news of Jesus work to change our *mindset* from alienation to freedom, from separation to reunion? (In other words, talk about the intellectual and emotional results of embracing the gospel.)

REMEMBER

"In the beginning was the Word, and the Word was with God, and the Word was God. . . . The Word became flesh and made his dwelling among us" (John 1:1, 14).

 HUDDLE

1. What do you sense God might be saying to you through the material discussed this week?

2. If your huddle group is open to it, take time to pray for each other, that we all might learn, live, and give the gospel.

NOTES

_____

_____

_____

_____

_____

_____

STUDY BUDDY TALKING POINTS

- God has something very important that he wants the world to hear, and it is summed up in the person and teaching of Jesus. Jesus is God's "Word" to us.

- The Bible says Jesus is Immanuel, which means "God with us." Jesus makes it abundantly clear that God is for us and not against us. Jesus embraced the people whom society rejected, and he forgave even his killers. This is God's heart toward all people. There is nothing we can do to make God give up on us.

- When we accept that Jesus is showing us God's heart, we can rest in the security of knowing that, even if we used to *think* God was against us ("enemies in our minds"), through Jesus we are reconciled to God and made "free from accusation."

- The message of Jesus has a miraculous quality to it. His teaching displays divine insight into our most fundamental human needs, and offers us a way to become the best version of ourselves. It's almost like the good news of Jesus is the perfect "owner's manual" for being human, written by our Manufacturer.

Jesus makes it abundantly clear that God is for us and not against us.

There is nothing we can do to make God give up on us.

NOTES

_____

_____

_____

_____

_____

_____

GOD'S GRAPHIC LOVE

Mapping the divine DNA

» Read chapter 7 of *Reunion* before this session «

👥 HANG OUT

We begin our discussion about the four *gifts* of the gospel (recall the graphic on p. 27) by zooming in on the message of God's love for us, which was made explicitly clear through the life and death and life again of Jesus.

We humans have an interesting problem. Whether consciously or unconsciously, we all long for *unconditional* love, to be fully embraced and accepted just as we are. But our observation and experience tell us that people rarely give and receive unconditional love. Our solution? We market a false version of ourselves to others in order to at least get *conditional* love. Hence, our true selves are rarely really known, or really loved.

Through Jesus, we learn about a God who completely *knows* us, even better than we know ourselves, and who completely *loves* us. Through Jesus we see that God's love for us is not only unconditional, like a gracious father's, but also instinctual, like a protective mother's. In other words, God cannot *not* love, because God *is* love (1 John 4:8, 16).

This also means that anything else that we perceive in God or receive from God—including justice, righteousness, and wrath—are all derivations and expressions of love.

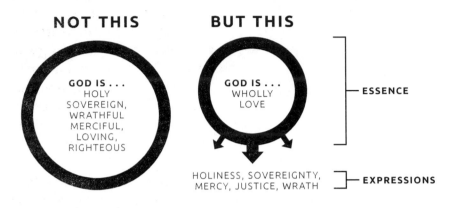

But isn't God more than mere love? I mean, don't we have to balance our picture of God's love with a healthy dose of, say, God's truth or wrath or justice or holiness or . . . ?

No. A thousand times no. We never "balance" God's love with some equal but opposite quality, like a yin to the yang. The yin-yang is not a Christian concept of God. God is love. Period. Everything else we say about God points to an expression of love.

God cannot not love, because God is love.

I once had a visitor to The Meeting House approach me after a Sunday service and ask with a tone that was as aggressive as it was inquisitive, "Are you a love church? Or a truth church?" I think I knew intuitively which he wanted me to answer, so I went with my gut and said, "We are definitely a truth

NOTES

_____

_____

_____

_____

_____

_____

church." Apparently, I had made the right choice, and the man smiled with relief. Then I added, "And we think the greatest truth is love."

The apostle John is the only writer of Scripture who dares declare the essence of the Almighty, and he does so three times:

God is *spirit*, says Jesus in John's gospel (John 4:24).

God *is light* (1 John 1:5).

God is *love* (1 John 4:8, 16).

The Bible describes God as having other qualities, expressions, and attributes, such as holiness, sovereignty, and righteousness. But these attributes are never described as God's *essence*. The essence of God is the spiritual light of love.

Now catch this: To say God is spirit, light, and love is to describe the same essence in three ways, and is not to say that God's essence is made up of three different substances or parts. There is not a "spirit" part of God, attached to the "light" part of God, next to the "love" part of God. God is 100 percent spirit, which is 100 percent light, which is 100 percent love.

This is worth establishing from the outset, because sometimes Christians do a silly thing and play one description of God's essence off another. They say things like, "Sure, God is pure love, but he is also pure light"—as though they have just pointed out something else in God that balances out his love. Most of the time they then go on to argue that the "light" of God refers to something like his holiness and white-hot wrath against sin. Now they have set themselves up to argue that God is love *and* wrath at his very core.

But the biblical texts don't support this. God is not love + anything. The spiritual light of God is love. God's love is light. God's light is pure

NOTES

_____

_____

_____

_____

_____

_____

No matter how we slice it, God is all spirit, all light, and all love.

spirit, which is pure love. No matter how we slice it, God is all spirit, all light, and all love.

As a test to make sure we're understanding the biblical concept of God correctly, try a simple thought experiment (similar to the one in chapter 3): Think back to before God created anything or anyone. Whatever is the essence or substance of God, it must be what God is apart from having created and before anyone or anything else existed. The essence of the Almighty is what God always is, including when God is all by himself.

Now we can test various qualities to see if they are on par with love: Is God's essence wrath? No, long before anyone or anything else existed, the Trinity were never mad at each other. Is God sovereignty? No, God is sovereign *over* and *in relation to* his creation, but the Trinity were never ruling over one another. Is God holiness? No again. To be holy means to be set apart: to be unlike what is common. And what could God be "set apart" from before he had created anything? Holiness as something intrinsic to God *before* he created is, in fact, a nonsensical concept. Of course, God is holy and forever will be holy now, because he has created. But holiness does not define God's divine DNA. God is pure spirit, and pure light, which is pure love.

We are talking about the essence of the Almighty. The DNA of the divine. The actual guts of God. We are, in a sense, standing on holy ground.

Only Jesus makes God's love unambiguous and crystal clear. We get mixed signals from nature, culture, and even Scripture until we allow the light of the Son to shine through it all. People may sense that God is

NOTES

_____

_____

_____

_____

_____

love. They may feel that God is love. They may theorize that God is love. But only Jesus shows us graphic evidence, etched into history itself, that God's essence is unrelenting, unconditional love.

Once we allow Jesus to fully convince our hearts that God really is love, we can embrace the fact that every experience we have of God is an expression of love (James 1:17). Now, keep in mind: not everything we experience comes from God. But everything that does come from God is an experience of love. Sometimes that love will be experienced as pure comfort (2 Corinthians 1:3-4). Other times God's love will come to us as corrective discipline (Proverbs 3:11-12; Hebrews 12:5-6). Still other times, when we are fighting back against God's best for our lives, that love may feel like hot coals poured on our heads (see Romans 12:20). Our experience of God's love will be determined by whether we embrace or reject it. But everything that comes to us from God will always be love.

When we let this sink in, our need for acceptance, affirmation, and belonging will be met supernaturally by God as our spiritual Parent, and by the family of faith into which we are adopted. Our compulsive drive to gain approval through performance or appearance can be laid aside. We will know we belong, rooted in a real and loving family and loved by the God we call *Abba*, which means "Daddy." We can then love others, not to gain their affection in return, but because we are already filled with love from God (1 John 4:19). When we allow ourselves to let go and fall into the embrace of our father God who loves us with a mother's heart (Isaiah 49:15), we will know who we are and whose we are. Once we clearly hear the God of the universe—who chose us before the world began and birthed us into being—say "I love you," we can love others out of our abundance rather than use others to gain the love we lack.

NOTES

ASK

1. What stood out to you from chapter 7 of *Reunion*, either as an encouragement, a challenge, a disagreement, or a question?
2. Jesus helps us see what true love is. How is this different from the idea of love that our culture most often celebrates?
3. How is God's love for us a "falling on a grenade" kind of love (pp. 87–88 in *Reunion*)? How is it even better?
4. How might you respond to a religious person who said, "Sure, God is love, but God is *also* . . . [insert any other quality here, such as sovereign judgment, righteous wrath, and so on]"?

WATCH

Take a few minutes to watch this brief video to help prepare you for this week's discussion.[1]

⫶⫶⫶ HEAR

It's time to hear from God through Scripture. Through Jesus we can "see" God's heart of love stamped into history. Through the Holy Spirit we can experience that love firsthand.

READ

Romans 5:5-11

[5] God's love has been poured out into our hearts through the Holy Spirit, who has been given to us.

---

1. bruxy.com/reunionstudy3

NOTES

_____

_____

_____

_____

_____

_____

6 You see, at just the right time, when we were still powerless, Christ died for the ungodly. **7** Very rarely will anyone die for a righteous person, though for a good person someone might possibly dare to die. **8** But God demonstrates his own love for us in this: While we were still sinners, Christ died for us.

9 Since we have now been justified by his blood, how much more shall we be saved from God's wrath through him! **10** For if, while we were God's enemies, we were reconciled to him through the death of his Son, how much more, having been reconciled, shall we be saved through his life! **11** Not only is this so, but we also boast in God through our Lord Jesus Christ, through whom we have now received reconciliation.

1 John 4:7-21

7 Dear friends, let us love one another, for love comes from God. Everyone who loves has been born of God and knows God. **8** Whoever does not love does not know God, because God is love. **9** This is how God showed his love among us: He sent his one and only Son into the world that we might live through him. **10** This is love: not that we loved God, but that he loved us and sent his Son as an atoning sacrifice for our sins. **11** Dear friends, since God so loved us, we also ought to love one another. **12** No one has ever seen God; but if we love one another, God lives in us and his love is made complete in us.

13 This is how we know that we live in him and he in us: He has given us of his Spirit. **14** And we have seen and testify that the Father has sent his Son to be the Savior of the world. **15** If anyone acknowledges that Jesus is the Son of God, God lives in them and they in God. **16** And so we know and rely on the love God has for us.

God is love. Whoever lives in love lives in God, and God in them. **17** This is how love is made complete among us so that we will have confidence on the day of judgment: In this world we are like Jesus. **18** There is no fear in love. But

NOTES

_____

_____

_____

_____

_____

_____

perfect love drives out fear, because fear has to do with punishment. The one who fears is not made perfect in love.

[19] We love because he first loved us. [20] Whoever claims to love God yet hates a brother or sister is a liar. For whoever does not love their brother and sister, whom they have seen, cannot love God, whom they have not seen. [21] And he has given us this command: Anyone who loves God must also love their brother and sister.

STUDY

1. What verse or idea stands out to you the most? Why?

2. Romantic love is usually drawn to something attractive in another person. How is God's love for us different? How is it similar?

3. How is God's love for us comparable to the story of the frog prince (pp. 93–94 in *Reunion*)? How does the Romans 5 passage support this?

4. Notice the apostle Paul's emphasis on reconciliation, or reunion. What are some of the things Jesus accomplishes to make this reunion possible?

5. The apostle John says our response to God's love should be to love others: "Dear friends, since God so loved us, we also ought to love one another" (1 John 4:11). Notice that he doesn't say that since God so loved us, we also ought to love God back. Instead, he insists that *we love God by loving others* (see the same theme in 1 John 3:16; Galatians 5:14; James 2:8; and Matthew 25:31-46). Without this emphasis, religion can sometimes cause people to show their love for God by pious pledges that lead to ignoring or even harming others. Talk about some examples of this in history and today.

NOTES

_____

_____

_____

_____

_____

_____

REMEMBER

"But God demonstrates his own love for us in this: While we were still sinners, Christ died for us" (Romans 5:8).

"Perfect love drives out fear" (1 John 4:18).

⌨ HUDDLE

1. What do you sense God might be saying to you through the material discussed this week?
2. If your huddle group is open to it, take time to pray for each other, that we all might learn, live, and give the gospel.

STUDY BUDDY TALKING POINTS

- Read this passage from the study guide to your study buddy (or let them read it) and invite their thoughts in response:

> We humans have an interesting problem. Whether consciously or unconsciously, we all long for *unconditional* love, to be fully embraced and accepted just as we are. But our observation and experience tell us that people rarely give and receive unconditional love. Our solution? We market a false version of ourselves to others in order to at least get *conditional* love. Hence, our true selves are rarely really known, or really loved.

Everything God does is an expression of love toward us.

NOTES

_____

_____

_____

_____

_____

_____

Through Jesus, we learn about a God who completely knows us, even better than we know ourselves, and who completely loves us. Through Jesus we see that God's love for us is not only unconditional, like a gracious father's, but also instinctual, like a protective mother's. In other words, God cannot *not* love, because God *is* love (1 John 4:8, 16).

- God is love. Most people who believe in God resonate with these three words, but only Jesus gives us the unambiguous evidence that this is true. (Talk about examples from the life and teachings of Jesus.)
- Love is not one of many attributes of God but the essence of the Almighty. This means that everything God does is an expression of love toward us. (But not everything we experience is from God.)
- In fact, we exist because God knew who we would be and loved us so much he chose to create us.
- Knowing this foundational truth meets our human need for belonging (See Maslow's chart on p. 28). We know who we are. We know *whose* we are. And we know where we belong, growing together as family.

NOTES

_____

_____

_____

_____

_____

_____

SEPARATION SOLUTION

Worth the price

» Read chapter 8 of *Reunion* before this session «

📇 HANG OUT

Our sins have separated us from God (Isaiah 59:1-2). In this session we're looking at the good news that God has gone to great lengths to remove our sin and bridge the gap.

Sometimes when religious people talk about sin and forgiveness, they approach the topic in a way that seems exquisitely designed to inflict maximum guilt and shame. "You are an utter failure in God's sight, a vile stench in the nostrils of a holy Sovereign, but because of his great mercy and forbearance, he has chosen to forgive you for the sake of his own glory." These kinds of preachers will often quote the prophet Isaiah saying, "All of us have become like one who is unclean, and all our righteous acts are like filthy rags" (Isaiah 64:6), suggesting that even our *good* deeds are considered bad by God. This approach ignores the immediate context, that Isaiah is confessing the rebellion and hypocrisy of his own people at that time. The verse just prior says that God helps those who gladly do right (some people do right!; also see Genesis 6:9; Job 1:1; and Luke 1:6), and confesses that God's people at that time were persecuting those who were trying to do right! So yes, they needed to hear that their "righteous acts" were not cutting it with God. But contrast this with the story in Acts 10 where a non-Christian Roman centurion named Cornelius is doing good deeds and an angel from God appears to him with a message. What is that message? Not "Stop trying to do good deeds! Don't you know they are like filthy rags to the Lord?" But rather, "Your prayers and gifts to the poor have come up as a memorial offering before God" (Acts 10:4).

So yes, we all sin and need God's forgiveness and reconciliation (Romans 3:23), but we don't have to pretend we are utterly devoid of any goodness in order to admit our need of a Savior. Jesus doesn't need us to feel horrible about ourselves so we can feel good about him. We *are* sinners. But we are also image-bearers of God. To see ourselves as subhuman worms is not humility; it is heresy. Jesus' message of forgiveness gives us an esteem rooted in the right things. And that's what this session is about.

Salvation and restoration of broken relationship is central to the message and mission of Jesus. The angel told Joseph to name his new foster son Jesus (which means "Yahweh saves") because "he will save his people from their sins" (Matthew 1:21). When Jesus grew up, he claimed that the reason he came into this world was "to seek and to save the lost" (Luke 19:10).

> *Jesus doesn't need us to feel horrible about ourselves so we can feel good about him.*

Through Christ's crucifixion, God does two things to save us from sin. Christian theologians give these two things very fancy words: *imputation* and *impartation*.

NOTES

First, God removes the record of our sin that condemns us before God as our judge. This is a kind of legal acquittal, like a judge declaring us not guilty. In theological terms, this is called *imputed* righteousness, or imputation. Now we are saved from God's wrath—that is, from having to face God as our judge with no defense against our guilt. Even if we know we are guilty of sin, the Judge of all has declared us righteous as far as he is concerned, which is really all that matters. If God himself declares me, a guilty sinner, to be innocent in his eyes, I'll happily accept his definition of reality with gratitude.

In fact, imputed righteousness is more than being declared innocent; it's more like the charges against us being completely thrown out of court. The apostle Paul writes that God "forgave us all our sins, having canceled the charge of our legal indebtedness, which stood against us and condemned us; he has taken it away, nailing it to the cross" (Colossians 2:13-14). When Christ died on the cross, he took the charge of our guilt, the law, with him. So the charges against us have been dropped. No matter who we are, if we're honest with ourselves, we know that we carry around with us a suitcase full of guilt over past "mistakes" we've made that have hurt people, including ourselves. Yet the good news of Jesus is that we are fully accepted by God because we are fully forgiven. And if we follow him, Jesus will mentor us in the art of forgiving others and ourselves.

Jesus will mentor us in the art of forgiving others and ourselves.

Now if this was all God did, we would be blessed enough. Still, our salvation might be a kind of "legal fiction"—like playing pretend that we are better than we actually are. So, at the risk of sounding like a 1980s TV commercial, it's important to say: *But wait! There's more!*

NOTES

God goes beyond *declaring* us righteous (imputation) and actually *makes* us righteous by healing our hearts and giving us his cleansing Spirit. Through the Hebrew prophet Ezekiel, God says, "I will sprinkle clean water on you, and you will be clean; I will cleanse you from all your impurities and from all your idols. I will give you a new heart and put a new spirit in you; I will remove from you your heart of stone and give you a heart of flesh" (Ezekiel 36:25-26). We may still be living in bodies that tempt us, brains that deceive us, and a world that misdirects us. But our souls, our hearts, our spiritual centers—who we really are—are totally healed. Theologians call this *imparted* righteousness, or impartation. Through the cleansing of Christ, the true me and the true you are made right with God.

The Protestant Reformation (c. 1517) was focused on and fueled by the idea of imputation: justification by faith alone. Many Protestant Christians today still emphasize imputation (being *declared* righteous) over impartation (being *made* righteous). Or they argue that impartation happens slowly, over time, via a process called sanctification. Martin Luther, for instance, is rumored to have said that justification (imputed righteousness) makes Christians like "snow-covered dung": the same on the inside, but covered with the righteousness of Christ on the outside.

On the other hand, the Radical Reformation (c. 1525) encouraged Christians to go beyond seeing themselves as merely *declared* righteous to seeing themselves as *being* truly righteous through God's grace. Today, these "Anabaptist" Christians (the faith family to which I belong) continue to stress the actual, inner change of heart that was promised to come with the new covenant (Ezekiel 36:26), and that is pictured through Jesus' idea of new birth and new creation (see John 3; 2 Corinthians 5:17-21). In theological terms, this moves us beyond "justification" to

NOTES

_____

_____

_____

_____

_____

"regeneration." Working with Luther's image, we could say that impartation actually reverses the metaphor: that is, Christians may still be covered in the "dung" of our sinful flesh, but on the inside—in our spirits, our true selves—we are pure and righteous and new.

So are we snow-covered dung or dung-covered snow? Both images are smelly and gross, so let's try a new metaphor. We could say that after we accept God's gift of salvation and rebirth into his family, our sinful impulses are more like leeches or parasites that attach themselves to us and try to manipulate us, but this is not our true self. We really are new!

This idea of being made new, of being "born again" as a new person with a fresh start (see John 3:3; 1 Peter 1:23), has powerful implications for how we think about ourselves. We are no longer sinful worms hoping for God's mercy. Nor are we morally neutral pawns with an angel on one shoulder and a devil on the other, each vying for our loyalty. Rather, in Christ we are completely new creations, made righteous and holy and perfectly loving. Our deepest affections have been reoriented and reinforced. Now our desire to make consistently loving choices is no longer viewed as a battle between equal but opposite internal forces (your good half versus your evil half). Rather, the struggle is between your real self and your false self, your spirit and your flesh, your inner person and your peripheral persona, your center and your circumference. This is why, even when he was aware of how often he failed, the apostle Paul could write that his real self did not sin: "Now if I do what I do not want to do, it is no longer I who do it, but it is sin living in me that does it" (Romans 7:20; see also v. 17). Once we are forgiven and justified and reborn through God's Spirit, sin is more like a foreign invader, an infection we fight against, rather than a characteristic that defines who we truly are.

NOTES

No other religion or philosophy or spiritual intervention strategy on the planet offers what the gospel of Jesus offers: God front-end loading a miracle. God personally cleanses us, enters us, and rebirths us into a renewed version of ourselves. Then God further equips us to make better choices through the ongoing guidance of his Spirit and the support of other Spirit-filled believers. Amazing! This means that the ethics of Jesus are based not just on our submission to God (i.e., "remember whose you are") but also on our actual identity (i.e., "remember who you are").

Why would God go to all this trouble and be so gracious toward us? Why become one of us and suffer alongside us? Why suffer all the more at our hand and on our behalf on the cross? Why take our sin onto himself and offer us his righteousness? Why pay so high a price for our salvation (Acts 20:28)?

God cleanses us, enters us, and rebirths us into a renewed version of ourselves.

Jesus makes this one thing abundantly clear: we matter to God, and he is not about to give up on us. In Luke 15, Jesus tells three stories about the lost being found: the parables of the lost coin, the lost sheep, and the lost son. And this is us. Think through human history and listen to what's in the news today and you'll have no trouble agreeing: we have lost our way. But something else is also true about the coin, the sheep, and the son. Each of these lost things is valuable to the one who has lost them, and worth searching for. That's how God thinks about you.

NOTES

_____

_____

_____

_____

_____

_____

ASK

1. What stood out to you from chapter 8 of *Reunion*, either as an encouragement, a challenge, a disagreement, or a question?

2. Sin is like an alien parasite that attaches itself to our brains and tries to manipulate our thoughts and feelings. Can you think of any science fiction movies that play with this theme?

We matter to God, and he is not about to give up on us.

3. "Sin separates us from who we were meant to be with *forever*" (p. 104 in *Reunion*). This chapter takes that sentence apart and builds it back together again bit by bit. What do you recall about each component?

   > Sin *separates*.
   > Sin separates *us*.
   > Sin separates us *from who we were*.
   > Sin separates us from who we were *meant to be*.
   > Sin separates us from who we were meant to be *with*.
   > Sin separates us from who we were meant to be with *forever*.

4. How does Jesus counter the separation referred to in each sentence?

WATCH

Take a few minutes to watch this brief video to help prepare you for this week's discussion.[1]

---

1. bruxy.com/reunionstudy4

NOTES

_____

_____

_____

_____

_____

_____

ᴵᴵᴵ HEAR

It's time to hear from God through Scripture. Reconnecting the detached, reuniting the separated, healing the broken, and reconciling the distant—this is a central theme of the gospel.

READ

2 Corinthians 5:17-21

[17] Therefore, if anyone is in Christ, the new creation has come: The old has gone, the new is here! [18] All this is from God, who reconciled us to himself through Christ and gave us the ministry of reconciliation: [19] that God was reconciling the world to himself in Christ, not counting people's sins against them. And he has committed to us the message of reconciliation. [20] We are therefore Christ's ambassadors, as though God were making his appeal through us. We implore you on Christ's behalf: Be reconciled to God. [21] God made him who had no sin to be sin for us, so that in him we might become the righteousness of God.

Ephesians 2:14-22

[14] For he himself is our peace, who has made the two groups one and has destroyed the barrier, the dividing wall of hostility, [15] by setting aside in his flesh the law with its commands and regulations. His purpose was to create in himself one new humanity out of the two, thus making peace, [16] and in one body to reconcile both of them to God through the cross, by which he put to death their hostility. [17] He came and preached peace to you who were far away and peace to those who were near. [18] For through him we both have access to the Father by one Spirit.

NOTES

_____

_____

_____

_____

_____

¹⁹ Consequently, you are no longer foreigners and strangers, but fellow citizens with God's people and also members of his household, ²⁰ built on the foundation of the apostles and prophets, with Christ Jesus himself as the chief cornerstone. ²¹ In him the whole building is joined together and rises to become a holy temple in the Lord. ²² And in him you too are being built together to become a dwelling in which God lives by his Spirit.

Colossians 1:21-23

²¹ Once you were alienated from God and were enemies in your minds because of your evil behavior. ²² But now he has reconciled you by Christ's physical body through death to present you holy in his sight, <u>without blemish and free from accusation</u>— ²³ if you continue in your faith, established and firm, and do not move from the hope held out in the gospel.

(Check out all of Colossians 1, a terrific chapter on God saving us from our sin. And while you're there, check out Colossians 3, a chapter that beautifully illustrates how Christians can and should make increasingly better choices, not just because of whose we are, but also because of who we are.)

STUDY

1. What verse or phrase stands out to you the most? Why?
2. Note that these passages speak of us being reconciled to God but never of God needing to be reconciled to us (this is consistent throughout the Bible). What does this tell us about ourselves? What does this tell us about God? Why is this distinction important?
3. Some Christians see their own identity this way: "I am still a rotten sinner, but thankfully when God looks upon me he sees me covered and clothed in the righteousness of Christ." How does

NOTES

_____

_____

_____

_____

_____

_____

the Scripture we've read push back against that understanding of what it means to be saved from sin?

4. The (re)union of the gospel is both vertical and horizontal. In Ephesians 2, the apostle Paul is writing about the severe division in the first century between Jews and Gentiles such as the Romans. He says that through Jesus, not only can enemies become friends; they can become family, and fellow citizens of a new unifying kingdom. What was the barrier dividing Jews and Gentiles, and how did Jesus get rid of it?

5. Do you think of yourself in terms of being an ambassador for Christ, carrying this message of reunion with God for others to hear? Why or why not?

REMEMBER

"God made him who had no sin to be sin for us, so that in him we might become the righteousness of God" (2 Corinthians 5:21).

 HUDDLE

1. What do you sense God might be saying to you through the material discussed this week?

2. As chapter 8 says, "Sin is a relationship disrupter. It separates people, divides groups, and fractures our own minds" (p. 101 in *Reunion*). How have you experienced the power of sin in your own life or in the lives of others?

3. If your huddle group is open to it, take time to pray for each other, that we all might learn, live, and give the gospel.

NOTES

_____

_____

_____

_____

_____

_____

STUDY BUDDY TALKING POINTS

- To sin means to separate, and it refers to anything we do to separate ourselves from loving relationship with God and others.
- Jesus brought us good news that God has wiped our slate clean and given us a fresh start. (That's called "justification.")
- But God does more than that. The gospel includes the good news that God wants to remake and renew us, healing our hearts and changing even our desires. (That's called "regeneration," or being "born again.")
- If we accept God's forgiveness and offer of reconciliation, God will also give us his Spirit to guide us so that we want more of what is good for us and less of what is damaging to ourselves and our relationships.
- The good news of forgiveness and salvation from our sin should encourage our hearts to know that God thinks we are worth pursuing (e.g., like the lost coin, lost sheep, and lost son).
- Rather than finding my self-esteem by pretending I'm better than I know I am, I can find my self-worth by trusting God's assessment of who I am: I am infinitely valuable because I am infinitely precious to the infinitely loving Creator of the universe.

NOTES

_____

_____

_____

_____

_____

OFF THE MAP

The purpose, place, and peace of the kingdom

» Read chapter 9 of *Reunion* before this session «

👥 HANG OUT

Up until now, we have studied the gospel as it is framed in most Christian churches: a message with an emphasis on God's gracious forgiveness for sin and salvation from judgment that we receive by faith. But for the next few sessions, we're going to discuss gospel themes that are underrepresented in many Christian circles: the kingdom of God, the irreligious implications of the new covenant, and our inclusion in God's love life.

This week, it's all about the kingdom baby! (That can be read two ways, I guess. It's all about the kingdom, baby! Or it's all about the kingdom baby, and that baby is Jesus. Hmm. Sometimes I overthink things.)

Jesus and the early church leaders most often framed their presentation of the gospel in terms of good news about God's kingdom (see, for example, Matthew 24:14; Acts 8:12; 28:31). That is, the good news of Jesus is the good news of the kingdom of God. This kingdom gospel is the good news that Jesus has brought about a new way of living together with God and one another in unity, harmony, and purpose.

Recall how we said that the gospel in thirty words connects with our most fundamental human needs. (See Hierarchy of Fundamental Needs chart, p. 28).

The gospel of the kingdom meets our human need for purpose and meaning in life.[1] In fact, we can state the ultimate purpose of every human being on earth in terms of the kingdom: *we exist on earth to experience and extend the kingdom of God.* This is why you are here, reading this, discussing together. Learning how to fulfill our kingdom purpose and helping others to do the same is the most meaningful thing we can do in this life.

> ## *We exist on earth to experience and extend the kingdom of God.*

A "kingdom" is a way of living in unity, rallied around the will and vision of one leader, a "king." In one sense, we are all kings or queens of our own micro-kingdoms. When we are children, our kingdom might be our bedroom, where our will and our way hold sway. When we are older, our kingdom might be our home, or our car or kitchen or office or art studio. At times, our kingdoms are invaded by others who overpower and enforce the will and way of another kingdom. Like when our parents punish us, or our housemates play their music too loud, or friends stay for a visit but don't respect our boundaries, or a neighbor's dog pees on our petunias. But Jesus teaches us that the only kingdom worth fighting for is his kingdom of love, and the only kingdom worth fighting against is the spiritual kingdom of darkness that works to divide all people from God and one another.

---

1. Again, this human need for purpose and meaning in life is the one thing we've added to Maslow's hierarchy of needs.

NOTES

_____

_____

_____

_____

_____

_____

The kingdom of God is a way of living in line with Jesus that brings his will and his way into this world more and more each day. People who follow Jesus are not just hoping for heaven when we die; we are part of God's project to bring heaven to earth

Jesus teaches us that the only kingdom worth fighting for is his kingdom of love.

right where we live. And that makes every day a day filled with purpose and meaning. Wherever we live and whatever we do, whomever we know and whomever we meet throughout our day, every moment is a moment of opportunity to live like citizens of and ambassadors for an alternate kingdom—the will and way of God that we were all made to experience and extend.

Humans were designed to be a part of something bigger than ourselves. We are made for that "something more" that is beyond us but that somehow includes us. We all know this, whether consciously or not. It is a truth we feel, like spiritual intuition.

Humans are like headphones, which find their created purpose only when they are plugged into a stereo. We are like books that are meant to be read, and instruments that are meant to be played. We come to life when we are connected and engaged with the "Something More" beyond but including ourselves.

The gospel of the kingdom reinforces that we have a sense of place. We are citizens together in a new community without division. In the book of Revelation, the apostle John has a vision of heavenly creatures singing praise to the Lamb with these words:

We are part of God's project to bring heaven to earth right where we live.

NOTES

_____

_____

_____

_____

_____

_____

You are worthy to take the scroll
    and to open its seals,
    because you were slain,
    and with your blood you purchased for God
    persons from every tribe and language and people and nation.
You have made them to be a kingdom and priests to serve our God,
    and they will reign on the earth.
(Revelation 5:9-10)

In a world torn apart by all kinds of divisions, the gospel of the kingdom meets one of our greatest personal and societal needs like nothing else. We belong together. We have a place and a people and a purpose: to experience and extend God's kingdom of peace.

ASK

1. What stood out to you from chapter 9 of *Reunion*, either as an encouragement, a challenge, a disagreement, or a question?

2. How often have you heard the gospel talked about in terms of the kingdom of God? In other words, how familiar are you with the themes in this chapter? Was there anything you hadn't thought of before?

3. Review the ten points of my response to Hank (pp. 127–28 in *Reunion*). Which points seem most or least convincing? Which points are new to you or most challenging to what you've heard from Christians before?

NOTES We oc here to conquer the space
between people. Pg 133.
Our struggle is not between flesh

WATCH

Take a few minutes to watch this brief video to help prepare you for this week's discussion.[2]

ᵃᵗˡᵗᵗˡᵗ HEAR

It's time to hear from God through Scripture. What does it mean to be a citizen of a country that is spiritual, relational, and borderless?

READ

Luke 13:18-19

18 What is the kingdom of God like? What shall I compare it to? **19** It is like a mustard seed, which a man took and planted in his garden. It grew and became a tree, and the birds perched in its branches.

What does it mean to be a citizen of a country that is spiritual, relational, and borderless?

Luke 17:20-21

20 The coming of the kingdom of God is not something that can be observed, **21** nor will people say, "Here it is," or "There it is," because the kingdom of God is in your midst.

---

2. bruxy.com/reunionstudy5

NOTES

_____

_____

_____

_____

_____

_____

Romans 10:9-17

9 If you declare with your mouth, "Jesus is Lord," and believe in your heart that God raised him from the dead, you will be saved. 10 For it is with your heart that you believe and are justified, and it is with your mouth that you profess your faith and are saved. 11 As Scripture says, "Anyone who believes in him will never be put to shame." 12 For there is no difference between Jew and Gentile—the same Lord is Lord of all and richly blesses all who call on him, 13 for, "Everyone who calls on the name of the Lord will be saved."

14 How, then, can they call on the one they have not believed in? And how can they believe in the one of whom they have not heard? And how can they hear without someone preaching to them? 15 And how can anyone preach unless they are sent? As it is written: "How beautiful are the feet of those who bring good news!"

16 But not all the Israelites accepted the good news. For Isaiah says, "Lord, who has believed our message?" 17 Consequently, faith comes from hearing the message, and the message is heard through the word about Christ.

STUDY

1. Jesus said the kingdom of God grows like a tiny mustard seed, which turns into a surprisingly large mustard plant. In fact, Jesus calls it a tree, which is a surprisingly bigger idea than the mustard bushes that mustard seeds usually grow into. This is miracle mustard vegetation! It's also worth noting that the symbol of birds often referred to pagan nations (think of the Roman eagle). So considering all of this, what does this parable tell us about how God's kingdom grows? Quickly or slowly? Organically or militaristically? Enemy-fighting or enemy-welcoming?

NOTES

2. Jesus said the kingdom of God *is* (not *will be*) within you (plural, not singular). In other words, the kingdom of God is between us as persons and within our relationships. It is, in Jesus' words, "in your midst" (Luke 17:21). Have you experienced the kingdom of God recently? Talk about examples.

3. How is "Jesus is Lord" a kingdom cry?

4. If you are a Christian, how does being a *citizen* of Christ's kingdom influence how you live? How does being an *ambassador* for this kingdom alter how you live?

5. Jesus began his kingdom manifesto, called the Sermon on the Mount (Matthew 5–7), with the words "Blessed are the poor in spirit, for theirs is the kingdom of heaven." What do you think it means to be someone who is poor in spirit? Why are they the first to receive the kingdom?

REMEMBER

"Blessed are the poor in spirit, for theirs is the kingdom of heaven" (Matthew 5:3).

 HUDDLE

1. What do you sense God might be saying to you through the material discussed this week?

2. If your huddle group is open to it, take time to pray for each other, that we all might learn, live, and give the gospel.

NOTES

_____

_____

_____

_____

_____

_____

STUDY BUDDY TALKING POINTS

- Jesus often referred to his message as "the good news of the kingdom of God." This doesn't mean Jesus was teaching us how to go to heaven when we die, though his gospel includes that. It means that Jesus was teaching us how to live in the flow of God's love in this life here and now.
- Jesus taught his followers to pray, "Thy kingdom come, thy will be done, on earth as it is in heaven."
- Demonstrate and explain the overlapping kingdom illustration from the video.
- All of this gives us a sense of purpose and place and peace in this world. Our purpose is to experience and extend the kingdom of God.

NOTES

REQUIEM FOR RELIGION

Out with the old, in with the new

» Read chapter 10 of *Reunion* before this session «

👥 HANG OUT

This is a session about the end of the old and the beginning of the new—covenant, that is. We cannot overstate this: Jesus changed the way humankind relates to God. "For the law was given through Moses; grace and truth came through Jesus Christ" (John 1:17). Or as the writer of Hebrews says, "By calling this covenant 'new,' he has made the first one obsolete; and what is obsolete and outdated will soon disappear" (Hebrews 8:13).

In some Christian circles, it is common to hear people say something like, "Christianity isn't about religion; it's about relationship." I think this is true. But I don't think most people have plumbed the depths of just how true it really is.

Having said that, people use words like *religion* and *religious* to mean different things. If you still struggle with the idea of using the word *religion* to refer to something that is anti-gospel, see my article "Is 'Religion' Good or Bad?" on my website, Bruxy.com.

For now, let's be clear: in this discussion, we're using the word *religion* to refer to a way of reaching out to God that is mediated through rules and rituals, holy people and holy places, such that these people, places, rituals, and rules become *necessary*. This is salvation by the system—a system that represents God to you and you to God.

Jesus, however, is God bypassing the system and coming directly to us. Jesus said, "I am the way" (John 14:6), and the apostle Paul wrote, "There is one God and one mediator between God and mankind, the man Christ Jesus, who gave himself as a ransom for all people" (1 Timothy 2:5-6).

Jesus replaces the laws of Moses with agape love as our guiding ethic. He replaces priests with the whole community of faith in which we are all priests to one another. He replaces holy buildings with the body of Christ, the family of faith, the people of God, who together form a living temple for God's Spirit to inhabit. And he replaces the many rituals of the old covenant with some simple practices, like baptism and communion, that don't *make* reality but *remind* us of what is already real. As Jesus said, "Do this in remembrance of me" (Luke 22:19).

In one sense, by establishing the new covenant God is helping humankind become who we were made to be. We are moving from letting God do all the thinking for us, so we can just obey his rules, to becoming students of Jesus, so he can mentor us in the art of making loving decisions for ourselves. This is what Abraham Maslow called "self-actualization." Self-actualization is the drive within all healthy humans to become all we were made to be; to transform all *potential* positive qualities into *actual* positive qualities. (See p. 21 of *Reunion* for more from Maslow.)

Sometimes we hear people talk about having an identity crisis or needing to "find themselves" or even just living with a nagging sense that

NOTES

there is some talent or potential within them that they need to develop in order to really become themselves. This inner ache has to do with self-actualization: turning our potential self into our actual self.

Before we are self-actualized, we will tend to identify ourselves primarily in terms of the roles we play—a spouse, a parent, a coworker, an artist, an actor, a leader, a lover, or more negatively, a failure, a screwup, a burden, a bum. But when we become self-actualized, we move beyond merely playing a role in life and begin making intentional choices out of our true identity.

Have you ever seen the movie *Forrest Gump?* As a young boy, Forrest is made to wear braces on his legs because of a crooked spine. At first the braces may have helped him, but little does he know that, after a while, those same braces are actually holding him back. The movie has an iconic scene in which some bullies are picking on Forrest and his friend Jenny tells him to run away. "Run, Forrest! Run!" she shouts, and he tries to run as fast as he can, which isn't very fast because of his leg braces. But eventually it happens—Forrest runs with such a sense of purpose and power that the braces bust and the pieces fall to the ground, allowing him to run faster and faster. Forrest has become the runner he was always meant to be.

Forrest Gump is a fictional character, but he represents something real for all of us. As the nonfictional character Eric Liddell says in the movie *Chariots of Fire,* "I believe God made me for a purpose, but he also made me fast. And when I run I feel his pleasure." When we become who we were meant to be, and live how we were meant to live, our souls will begin to experience the pleasure of God.

Under the old covenant, the rituals and rules functioned like spiritual braces, designed to help our malformed souls move forward with God at a pace we could handle. God knew that our internal selves lacked the

NOTES

willpower or the confidence or the courage or the humility to walk and talk with God as friends, so God met us where we were at. God tried the face to face, heart to heart approach while relating with his people, but we refused and asked God to speak through Moses as a mediator (see Exodus 20:18-19). Then, while God was revealing his will to Moses, the people of God got it on with a golden calf. Humankind had a lot of growing up to do.

But now, through the new covenant, God strengthens our souls by giving us a new heart and filling us with his own Spirit. We don't need the braces anymore. Now we can walk and run and dance with God as friends, because "those who hope in the Lord will renew their strength. They will soar on wings like eagles; they will run and not grow weary, they will walk and not be faint" (Isaiah 40:31).

The new covenant is the self-actualization of humanity. Living in (re)union with God, we no longer make ethical decisions by asking, "What is the rule for this situation?" Rather, we ask, "Who am I, and how am I made to live?" The answer to that question will always be that we are God's precious image-bearers, and we were made to live a life of Jesus-like love. Now when faced with an ethical challenge, we no longer ask, "What does the rulebook say?" but "What does love look like in this situation?"

Old covenant ethics were based on the idea of reward and punishment: Do this and you will be rewarded. Don't do that, or you will be punished. New covenant ethics work from the inside out. God gives us a new heart, his own Spirit, the example of Jesus, the teaching of Scripture, and the support of other believers. Then God says, "Do whatever you want"—knowing that what we really want is changing and realigning with who we were always meant to be.

By God's grace, we are becoming ourselves.

NOTES

ASK

1. What stood out to you from chapter 10, either as an encouragement, a challenge, a disagreement, or a question?
2. People use the words *spirituality* and *religion* differently. Do you tend to use the word *religion* to refer to something positive or negative?
3. Just before Jesus died on the cross, he cried out, "It is finished!" What was finished?
4. Through his crucifixion, Jesus became all three elements of the sacrificial religion of his day: the temple, the priest, and the sacrifice. Talk about the ways that Jesus' followers, the body of Christ, have now become each of these three things together.
5. In what ways is grace a powerfully irreligious concept?

WATCH

Take a few minutes to watch this brief video to help prepare you for this week's discussion.[1]

HEAR

It's time to hear from God through Scripture. A little toddler benefits from rules and routines to help him or her be safe, feel secure, and grow wise. Even if the child is heir to an estate, he or she is still told what to do and when to do it while still a young child. But when the child grows up and becomes a young man or woman, the inheritance becomes truly their own, and that heir rises above the rules and routines of childhood.

1. bruxy.com/reunionstudy6

NOTES

The apostle Paul uses this analogy to help us understand the difference between old and new covenant living.

READ

Galatians 3:23–4:7

23 Before the coming of this faith, we were held in custody under the law, locked up until the faith that was to come would be revealed. 24 So the law was our guardian until Christ came that we might be justified by faith. 25 Now that this faith has come, we are no longer under a guardian.

26 So in Christ Jesus you are all children of God through faith, 27 for all of you who were baptized into Christ have clothed yourselves with Christ. 28 There is neither Jew nor Gentile, neither slave nor free, nor is there male and female, for you are all one in Christ Jesus. 29 If you belong to Christ, then you are Abraham's seed, and heirs according to the promise.

4:1 What I am saying is that as long as an heir is underage, he is no different from a slave, although he owns the whole estate. 2 The heir is subject to guardians and trustees until the time set by his father. 3 So also, when we were underage, we were in slavery under the elemental spiritual forces of the world. 4 But when the set time had fully come, God sent his Son, born of a woman, born under the law, 5 to redeem those under the law, that we might receive adoption to sonship. 6 Because you are his sons,[2] God sent the Spirit of his Son into our hearts, the Spirit who calls out, "*Abba*, Father." 7 So you are no longer a slave, but God's child; and since you are his child, God has made you also an heir.

---

2. Calling all God's children his "sons" might sound exclusionary toward women, but the opposite is true here. Back in biblical times, only sons could receive an inheritance. Daughters got nothing. To say that men and women could all become God's "sons" was a way of championing equality. That is, both women and men could equally look forward to the full blessings of inheritance from God.

NOTES

_____

_____

_____

_____

_____

_____

STUDY

1. What verse or idea stands out to you?

2. Drawing from this passage, how would you respond to someone who asked, "If God always intended to send Jesus to show us this new covenant way, why did he set up the law of Moses in the first place?"

3. Paul uses the analogy of the Old Testament law being like a kind of prison. In what ways does prison benefit a person and a society? How does it hinder a person or a society? Discuss how this relates to the idea of religious law.

4. The apostle Paul says that the old covenant law functioned in our lives like a kind of "guardian" (the original Greek word here is *paidagogos*, which refers to a kind of nanny, caretaker, or babysitter for young children). In what ways was the law of Moses like a caretaker for the Hebrew people? Why don't we need it to govern our lives today?

5. Sometimes the Bible speaks of us being reborn into God's family, and here the apostle Paul talks about us being adopted by God. Either way, no one *works* their way into a family. It is pure grace. What aspects of being God's child does adoption help to highlight?

REMEMBER

"God sent the Spirit of his Son into our hearts, the Spirit who calls out, '*Abba*, Father'" (Galatians 4:6).

NOTES

_____

_____

_____

_____

_____

_____

💬 HUDDLE

1. What do you sense God might be saying to you through the material discussed this week?
2. If your huddle group is open to it, take time to pray for each other, that we all might learn, live, and give the gospel.

STUDY BUDDY TALKING POINTS

- The Bible uses the word *covenant* to refer to a way of being in relationship. Through the "old covenant" (the part before Jesus), God related to humankind through rules and rituals (like the Ten Commandments and animal sacrifices).
- Jesus claimed to inaugurate the "new covenant": a way of relating to God and each other based on love rather than law, trust rather than tradition.
- On the cross, Jesus fulfilled and ended the entire religious system of his day—and that of our day too. Jesus became the last sacrifice, the temple where the sacrifice is offered, and the high priest who offers the sacrifice, once for all.
- The good news of Jesus includes this message of pure grace. Grace means God giving us, as a gift, everything religion tries but fails to accomplish.
- In the new covenant, God also offers us his Holy Spirit to partner with our hearts to help us become the best version of ourselves.
- All of this meets our human need for self-actualization—becoming our true selves.

NOTES

GOD'S LOVE LIFE

You need to get out more

» Read chapter 11 of *Reunion* before this session «

👥 HANG OUT

In this session we're talking about the *goal* of the gospel: intimacy with the Almighty—that is, embracing and being embraced by the triune love life of God. The apostle Peter spoke about our privilege to "participate in the divine nature" (2 Peter 1:4). This is what theologians call *theosis*, or (re)union with God.

During the last session we discussed how the new covenant removes the old braces of law and helps us grow into the new way of love. This is very similar to what Abraham Maslow called self-actualization, or becoming our actual selves, the selves we were made to be.

Most first-year psychology textbooks today show an earlier version of Maslow's hierarchy of needs that keeps self-actualization at the top of the pyramid as the ultimate goal of human development. This says more about the bias of the mental health and education professions than it does about the true nature of human need, or even about Maslow's final thoughts on the matter. You see, after years of testing his theory,

Maslow revised his thinking, claiming that human need goes beyond self-*actualization* to self-*transcendence*. (See p. 21 of *Reunion*.)

Maslow revised his theory after continued research revealed that people who experience self-actualization without moving on to self-transcendence can get stuck in the practice of pursuing their own fulfillment. In other words, people who pursue self-actualization but who never reach out beyond themselves can become increasingly narcissistic. In fact, Maslow noted that people who fail to experience some form of self-transcendence will be more likely to experience some form of "metapathology" such as apathy, cynicism, boredom, despair, or nihilism. This is fascinating, since the Bible records examples of people in the early church who got stuck at this level and saw the new covenant message of grace as their license to live sinful, selfish lives (see the apostle Paul's first letter to the Corinthians for some examples).

Contrasted to this, people who become what Maslow called "transcenders" are characterized by outward- and upward-looking qualities. Maslow listed many traits, but here are five examples:

1. Transcenders are motivated by something beyond "their own skin"; that is, they care about more than just their own self-interest.
2. They can be both more happy and more sad about the world. This emotional state is actually in keeping with reality, since there is more to be happy *and* sad about in this world than most of us let on.
3. They experience a positive correlation between knowledge (simply learning new things), on the one hand, and awe, mystery, humility, and reverence, on the other.

NOTES

4. They find the world fascinating, the way children do, and "get hypnotized by the colors in a puddle, or by the raindrops dripping down a windowpane, or by the smoothness of skin, or the movements of a caterpillar."

5. They experience and express "wholehearted and unconflicted love."[1]

Amazingly, while Maslow believed other needs must be met in a set order (e.g., we must meet our physical needs before we can focus on belonging, and must have our esteem needs met before we can move on to self-actualization), his research led him to conclude that anyone at any time can experience and benefit from self-transcendence. People who are starving to death can feel close to God. Others who lack safety because they are being persecuted for their faith can experience intimacy with God as they choose to lay down their lives for others. No matter what our current circumstance, we can all get out of ourselves now and begin to experience self-transcendence.

There are basically two ways we can self-transcend: *up* and *out*. Transcending *up* means reaching beyond ourselves to connect with God directly through means like prayer, nature, Scripture study, meditation, and what psychologists call "peak experiences": simply waking up to an awareness of God's presence all around us, or what Brother Lawrence, a seventeenth-century monk, called "practicing the presence of God." Transcending *out* means reaching beyond ourselves to serve and love and meet the needs of other people around us—what could be called "practicing the presence of people."

---

1. From Maslow's landmark 1969 article "Theory Z," reprinted in A. H. Maslow, *The Farther Reaches of Human Nature* (New York: Viking, 1972), 282.

NOTES

When we transcend out in love, we also transcend up in worship.

In his story of the sheep and the goats (Matthew 25:31-46), Jesus shows us how to do both at the same time. Jesus teaches that when we reach out beyond ourselves to honor others around us by actively meeting their immediate needs, we are honoring *him*. When we serve the hungry and thirsty and lonely and naked and sick and imprisoned, we are serving *Jesus*. In other words, when we transcend *out* in love, we are simultaneously transcending *up* in worship.

So self-transcendence can begin here and now through simple acts of compassion, kindness, and other-centered love, and it can stretch on into an eternal intimacy with the Almighty. The apostle Paul wrote, "Since, then, you have been raised with Christ, set your hearts on things above, where Christ is, seated at the right hand of God. Set your minds on things above, not on earthly things. For you died, and your life is now hidden with Christ in God" (Colossians 3:1-3). When Paul says we should set our hearts and minds on things above, he doesn't mean that we should think about heaven only and ignore the world around us. Rather, Paul is inviting us to see *this* world differently, as the beginning of our eternal life. We can see "things above" all around us in this world, rather than getting distracted by "earthly things" that miss the bigger picture.

Jesus connects eternal life with intimate life when he says to the Father in prayer, "Now this is eternal life: that they know you, the only true God, and Jesus Christ, whom you have sent" (John 17:3). In this verse, "knowing" means an intimate, experiential knowledge. May we always be growing in knowing God, in this life, and in the life to come, a time when we will know fully, even as we are already fully known (1 Corinthians 13:12).

NOTES

_____

_____

_____

_____

_____

_____

ASK

1. What stood out to you from chapter 11, either as an encouragement, a challenge, a disagreement, or a question?

> *The goal of the gospel is embracing and being embraced by the triune love life of God.*

2. Chapter 11 suggests that "what we call heaven is less of a *place* and more of a *Person*" (p. 165 in *Reunion*). What do you think about that?

3. The goal of the gospel is not the *rejection* of our bodies, but the *redemption* of our bodies (Romans 8:23), not a *release* from the physical but a *resurrection* to a renewed version of our physical selves, of which Jesus is the prototype. God values the physical! What are some implications of this for how we live today?

4. The Bible uses two metaphors to talk about the way we become God's children and dearly loved members of his family: birth (John 3:3; 1 Peter 1:3-4) and adoption (Romans 8:14-17; Galatians 4:1-7). What are some unique and beautiful truths that each metaphor communicates?

5. Have you ever had your own "incubator of agape" experience (pp. 178–80 in *Reunion*)? How could local churches do a better job of providing this for hurting people?

WATCH

Take a few minutes to watch this brief video to help prepare you for this week's discussion.[2]

---

2. bruxy.com/reunionstudy7

NOTES

⑾⑾ HEAR

It's time to hear from God through Scripture. While Buddhism speaks about the value of *detachment*, Jesus teaches the way of heightened *attachment*—to the love life of God.

READ

John 14:15-20

[15] If you love me, keep my commands. [16] And I will ask the Father, and he will give you another advocate to help you and be with you forever— [17] the Spirit of truth. The world cannot accept him, because it neither sees him nor knows him. But you know him, for he lives with you and will be in you. [18] I will not leave you as orphans; I will come to you. [19] Before long, the world will not see me anymore, but you will see me. Because I live, you also will live. [20] On that day you will realize that I am in my Father, and you are in me, and I am in you.

John 14:23

Anyone who loves me will obey my teaching. My Father will love them, and we will come to them and make our home with them.

John 15:15

I no longer call you servants, because a servant does not know his master's business. Instead, I have called you friends, for everything that I learned from my Father I have made known to you.

John 17:26

I have made you known to them, and will continue to make you known in order that the love you have for me may be in them and that I myself may be in them.

NOTES

_____

_____

_____

_____

_____

_____

Galatians 2:20
I have been crucified with Christ and I no longer live, but Christ lives in me. The life I now live in the body, I live by faith in the Son of God, who loved me and gave himself for me.

2 Peter 1:3-4
³ His divine power has given us everything we need for a godly life through our knowledge of him who called us by his own glory and goodness. ⁴ Through these he has given us his very great and precious promises, so that through them you may participate in the divine nature, having escaped the corruption in the world caused by evil desires.

Revelation 21:22
I did not see a temple in the city, because the Lord God Almighty and the Lamb are its temple.

STUDY

1. One of the ways we live out our love for Jesus is to obey his teaching (i.e., "If you love me, keep my commands."). Brainstorm: What are some examples of the plain teachings of Jesus that we should obey?

2. How is the image of God himself being the temple both shockingly irreligious and beautifully intimate?

3. Read the following statements and talk about what that might look like after we die, and before we die, starting today.
   - "Whoever hears my word and believes him who sent me has eternal life and will not be judged but has crossed over from death to life" (John 5:24; see also 6:47).

NOTES

_____

_____

_____

_____

_____

- "On that day you will realize that I am in my Father, and you are in me, and I am in you" (John 14:20).
- "We will come to them and make our home with them" (John 14:23).
- "I have called you friends" (John 15:15).
- "In order that the love you have for me may be in them and that I myself may be in them" (John 17:26).
- "Christ lives in me" (Galatians 2:20).
- "Your life is now hidden with Christ in God" (Colossians 3:3).
- "He has given us his very great and precious promises, so that through them you may participate in the divine nature" (2 Peter 1:4).

4. Sometimes people say things like, "The true nature of the universe is that there is no distinction between anyone and anything. There is no you and no me, no spoon and no tree. We are all one." How does this differ from the worldview of Jesus? Which view is most conducive to love?

REMEMBER
"I have called you friends" (John 15:15).

 HUDDLE

1. What do you sense God might be saying to you through the material discussed this week?
2. If your huddle group is open to it, take time to pray for each other, that we all might learn, live, and give the gospel.

NOTES

_____

_____

_____

_____

_____

_____

STUDY BUDDY TALKING POINTS

- God is love. And God's goal for our lives is to live in love with God. This includes eternal life eventually and abundant life starting right now.

We are invited into the love life of God.

- We are invited into the love life of God, to participate in the relationship of the Trinity, allowing God's love to come to us and pass through us on to others.
- Participating in the love life of God fulfills our need for self-transcendence.
- Unless we grow to connect beyond ourselves, we can become stuck in a stage of development that is focused on our own well-being to the point of selfish self-obsession.
- We transcend *up* through our intimate connection with God (e.g., prayer, meditation, Scripture study, musical praise, practicing the presence of God). We transcend *out* through our loving service of others (e.g., attitudes of honor, deeds of kindness, practicing the presence of people).

NOTES

_____

_____

_____

_____

_____

_____

THE F-WORD AND SO WHAT?

Selling it all to buy a field

» Read chapter 12 and the epilogue before this session «

🫂 HANG OUT

You've made it to the last session! Way to invest your time in what is most important: the good news of Jesus, for seekers, saints, and sinners. Hugs, high fives, and hurrays all around!

This time we're wrapping things up by looking at our own lives. Where do we stand in relation to Jesus? One of the words the Bible uses to refer to being in right relationship with God is *righteousness.* Today we might think of a "righteous" person as someone who lives a morally exemplary life—or, on the other hand, as someone who is snobbishly pious in all the worst ways. The gospel is the good news that we'll never be good enough for God—wait, why is that good news? Because God has offered us his own righteousness as a gift, not a wage. The pressure is off. All we have to do is trust that this is true, and we shed our spiritual anxiety and welcome God's salvation as the free gift that it is. In response to the question of what we have to *do* for God—What *work* must we do for God in order to *earn* salvation as a wage for services rendered?—Jesus responds, "The work of God is this: to believe in the one he has sent" (John 6:29).

When teaching, Jesus revealed deep truths through simple stories called parables. They are sometimes short and are designed to convey a powerful point through a single image. For instance, here is one of my favorites on the themes of grace, faith, salvation, and the kingdom:

> The kingdom of heaven is like treasure hidden in a field. When a man found it, he hid it again, and then in his joy went and sold all he had and bought that field. (Matthew 13:44)

That's it! Short and sweet, yet it says so much. For instance:

The kingdom of heaven is so precious that it is worth giving up everything we already own.

First, the kingdom of heaven is like hidden treasure—it doesn't leap out at you and hit you in the face, but it reveals itself to those who are looking.

Second, to raise the money to buy the field, the man sold all he had. We must be convinced that this treasure of the kingdom of heaven is so precious that it is worth giving up everything we already own. This might mean giving up different kinds of things for each of us: people (unhealthy relationships), possessions (the stuff that holds us back from what is most important), places (going to places, getting into situations, and participating in activities that do not bring out the best in us), or pride (an attitude of self-sufficiency or smugness that keeps us from the humble cry, "I need God!"). In the words of Jim Elliot, "He is no fool who gives what he cannot keep to gain that which he cannot lose."[1]

---

1. *The Journals of Jim Elliot,* edited by Elisabeth Elliot (Grand Rapids, MI: Revell, 1978), 174.

NOTES

_____

_____

_____

_____

_____

_____

Third, the treasure of life with God is free. This is an ironic truth, because the field is costly. The man had to liquidate all his assets to afford the field. But don't miss his motivation: this purchase was sheer privilege, because it came with an infinitely precious treasure that neither he nor we could ever afford. Whatever we give up, leave behind, or lay aside to follow Jesus is pure privilege, because in doing so, we receive God's gift of salvation that we could never purchase by a lifetime of being diligent do-gooders. The infinitely unaffordable treasure is really all ours when we purchase the field.

Lastly, the man sold all he had and bought the field "in his joy." Joy is at the heart of the kingdom. Giving up what is temporary to begin our eternal life now is not dull deprivation or dreary drudgery. Yes, we may choose to give up many things

The treasure of life with God is free.

that provide us with short-lived, temporary, transient joy, including possessions, hobbies, habits, and relationships that don't align with the kingdom. But the reward of an ever-expanding relationship with God and with a new family that stretches around the world and back through time is the far greater happiness. In the words of Tony Campolo, "The kingdom of God is a party!"[2]

ASK

1. What stood out to you from chapter 12 and the epilogue, either as an encouragement, a challenge, a disagreement, or a question?
2. Mark Twain wrote, "Faith is believing what you know ain't so." In other words, having faith is just playing pretend about spiritual

2. Tony Campolo, *The Kingdom of God Is a Party: God's Radical Plan for His Family* (Nashville, Thomas Nelson, 1990).

NOTES

_____

_____

_____

_____

_____

_____

things to comfort ourselves, when really we all know better. What do you think?

3. Think back to when you first started reading *Reunion*. How have your ideas about God and the gospel changed, grown, or been reinforced?
4. What do you sense God might be saying to you through the material discussed this week?

WATCH

Take a few minutes to watch this brief video to help prepare you for this week's discussion.[3]

HEAR

It's time to hear from God through Scripture. We're going to work through an entire chapter of Jesus' teaching, Luke 15, which contains three stories about being lost and found.

READ

Luke 15

1 Now the tax collectors and sinners were all gathering around to hear Jesus.
2 But the Pharisees and the teachers of the law muttered, "This man welcomes
sinners and eats with them."

3 Then Jesus told them this parable: 4 "Suppose one of you has a hundred
sheep and loses one of them. Doesn't he leave the ninety-nine in the open
country and go after the lost sheep until he finds it? 5 And when he finds it, he

3. bruxy.com/reunionstudy8/

NOTES

joyfully puts it on his shoulders **6** and goes home. Then he calls his friends and neighbors together and says, 'Rejoice with me; I have found my lost sheep.' **7** I tell you that in the same way there will be more rejoicing in heaven over one sinner who repents than over ninety-nine righteous persons who do not need to repent.

8 "Or suppose a woman has ten silver coins and loses one. Doesn't she light a lamp, sweep the house and search carefully until she finds it? **9** And when she finds it, she calls her friends and neighbors together and says, 'Rejoice with me; I have found my lost coin.' **10** In the same way, I tell you, there is rejoicing in the presence of the angels of God over one sinner who repents."

11 Jesus continued: "There was a man who had two sons. **12** The younger one said to his father, 'Father, give me my share of the estate.' So he divided his property between them.

13 "Not long after that, the younger son got together all he had, set off for a distant country and there squandered his wealth in wild living. **14** After he had spent everything, there was a severe famine in that whole country, and he began to be in need. **15** So he went and hired himself out to a citizen of that country, who sent him to his fields to feed pigs. **16** He longed to fill his stomach with the pods that the pigs were eating, but no one gave him anything.

17 "When he came to his senses, he said, 'How many of my father's hired servants have food to spare, and here I am starving to death! **18** I will set out and go back to my father and say to him: Father, I have sinned against heaven and against you. **19** I am no longer worthy to be called your son; make me like one of your hired servants.' **20** So he got up and went to his father.

"But while he was still a long way off, his father saw him and was filled with compassion for him; he ran to his son, threw his arms around him and kissed him.

21 "The son said to him, 'Father, I have sinned against heaven and against you. I am no longer worthy to be called your son.'

NOTES

_____

_____

_____

_____

_____

_____

²² "But the father said to his servants, 'Quick! Bring the best robe and put it on him. Put a ring on his finger and sandals on his feet. ²³ Bring the fattened calf and kill it. Let's have a feast and celebrate. ²⁴ For this son of mine was dead and is alive again; he was lost and is found.' So they began to celebrate.

²⁵ "Meanwhile, the older son was in the field. When he came near the house, he heard music and dancing. ²⁶ So he called one of the servants and asked him what was going on. ²⁷ 'Your brother has come,' he replied, 'and your father has killed the fattened calf because he has him back safe and sound.'

²⁸ "The older brother became angry and refused to go in. So his father went out and pleaded with him. ²⁹ But he answered his father, 'Look! All these years I've been slaving for you and never disobeyed your orders. Yet you never gave me even a young goat so I could celebrate with my friends. ³⁰ But when this son of yours who has squandered your property with prostitutes comes home, you kill the fattened calf for him!'

³¹ "'My son,' the father said, 'you are always with me, and everything I have is yours. ³² But we had to celebrate and be glad, because this brother of yours was dead and is alive again; he was lost and is found.'"

STUDY

1. What was the motive of Jesus to tell these three stories? Who was his audience, and what was Jesus responding to?
2. What do you see in these stories that reflects God's love for individuals and not just a generic love for humankind in general?
3. Look at the theme of joy and rejoicing in the first two stories (the lost sheep and lost coin). Who is happy? Who does the joyful person represent? How does that make you feel?
4. What thought motivated the prodigal son to go home? In what ways was his image of his father accurate but incomplete? Do you think God is better than you imagine?

NOTES

5. Where does the wrath of God appear in any of these stories? What does it look like?

6. How does the father greet the son who returns home? What does that tell us about God?

Grace is God giving us salvation as a gift. Faith is us reaching up to receive this gift.

7. Why was the older brother upset? Who does he represent in the story?

8. How do you think Jesus' original audience responded to these stories?

9. Where would you say you are in your spiritual journey? Far from God in a distant country? Standing in the field, frustrated with your father? Coming to your senses? Feeling your father's embrace? In the middle of the party? Somewhere else?

REMEMBER

"When he came near the house, he heard music and dancing" (Luke 15:25).

 HUDDLE

1. What do you sense God might be saying to you through the material discussed this week? What next step do you think you could take in your spiritual journey? (Review the "Now what?" options on pp. 204–207 of *Reunion*.)

2. If your huddle group is open to it, take time to pray for each other, that we all might learn, live, and give the gospel.

NOTES

_____

_____

_____

_____

_____

_____

STUDY BUDDY TALKING POINTS

- We no longer do religious things to earn salvation. The Jesus-led life is one filled with celebration of what we already are and have been given.
- Christians are those peculiar people who gather together every Sunday to celebrate the fact that we don't *have* to gather together every Sunday to be saved. We read the Bible regularly to be reminded of the good news that we don't *have* to read the Bible regularly to be right with God. We sing songs of worship to express our adoration for the One who says we don't *have* to sing, or pray, or meditate, or participate in any liturgy in order to be on God's good side.
- Grace is God giving us salvation as a gift. Faith is us reaching up to receive this gift.
- Thank you for making it all the way to the end of this experiment! You are most gracious! What do you think about this good news message of Jesus?
- Even if you're not sure if there is a God, the next step for you might be prayer. When you enter a house and you wonder if anybody is home, one of the best ways to find out is to call out, "Hello? Is there anybody here?" Would you be willing to pray to ask God to reveal himself to you further? Either way, I'll be praying for you.

NOTES

LEARNING, LIVING, AND GIVING THE GOSPEL

Learning

We've spent a significant amount of time *learning* the gospel together. Your feedback can help me learn too, especially about how to improve this book study. What truths have made the most impact? What questions have gone unanswered? I'd love to hear from you. You can email me at bruxy@bruxy.com, or look for me on social media—with a name like mine I should be easy to find!

Living

Take time to picture how your life and the lives of others who embrace the good news of Jesus will be different when we live as though these things are true:

- God is for us and not against us.
- God values us with an infinite and intimate love.

- God has already forgiven us for any failure and wants to pull us closer.
- God has given our lives meaning as citizens of and ambassadors for his kingdom of peace.
- God has given us all of this as a gift of grace, without any pressure to perform.
- God's goal for our lives, starting now and stretching into eternity, is the experience of ongoing and increasing intimacy with God's very own love life.

I hope you see that the gospel has the potential to transform how we live here and now, and not just offer us the promise of heaven when we die.

Giving

The good news of Jesus for seekers, saints, and sinners is too good to keep to ourselves. To do so would be unloving. Faith is always personal but never private. Faith is always relational, and faith in Jesus is a relationship that is meant to be shared through our relationships.

"The Maple Leafs won the Stanley Cup!" might be unbelievably good news to Torontonians, causing them to cheer while jumping up and down for hours (or simply to faint on the spot from the sheer shock of this unlikely event). But regardless of how Torontonians react, it is a rather irrelevant message for most of the world. On the other hand, the good news of Jesus is *the* most relevant message for every person on this planet. When embraced, the gospel brings people into a global celebration that stretches around the world, back through time, and into an

NOTES

infinite future. This is a message worth sharing. (And the "understatement of the year" award goes to—may I have the envelope please!—that last sentence!)

So let's give the final word to Jesus, who blessed and commissioned his followers with these last words: "All authority in heaven and on earth has been given to me. Therefore go and make disciples of all nations, baptizing them in the name of the Father and of the Son and of the Holy Spirit, and teaching them to obey everything I have commanded you. And surely I am with you always, to the very end of the age" (Matthew 28:18-20).

NOTES

_____

_____

_____

_____

_____

_____